Jim McCullough
2211 H St.
B'ham, Wash

LL 175

Plate 1 Plants and water.

The Institute of Biology's
Studies in Biology no. 14

Plants and Water

by *James Sutcliffe* D.Sc., Ph.D., F.I.Biol.
Professor of Plant Physiology, University of Sussex

Edward Arnold (Publishers) Ltd

First published 1968
Reprinted 1969

Boards edition SBN : 7131 2209 9
Paper edition   SBN : 7132 2210 2

Printed in Great Britain by
William Clowes and Sons Ltd, London and Beccles

General Preface to the Series

It is no longer possible for one textbook to cover the whole field of Biology and to remain sufficiently up to date. At the same time students at school, and indeed those in their first year at universities, must be contemporary in their biological outlook and know where the most important developments are taking place.

The Biological Education Committee, set up jointly by the Royal Society and the Institute of Biology, is sponsoring, therefore, the production of a series of booklets dealing with limited biological topics in which recent progress has been most rapid and important.

A feature of the series is that the booklets indicate as clearly as possible the methods that have been employed in elucidating the problems with which they deal. There are suggestions for practical work for the student which should form a sound scientific basis for his understanding.

1967

INSTITUTE OF BIOLOGY
41 Queen's Gate
London, S.W.7

Preface

At first sight, plant–water relations seem to be among the more straightforward aspects of plant physiology, and partly for this reason perhaps they are often most difficult for students to grasp. Matters have not been helped in the past by use of confusing terms, of which 'suction pressure' is perhaps the classic example. In this booklet a new terminology based on thermodynamic concepts is used in the hope that it will help students to understand more clearly the physical principles underlying water movement in plants.

My thanks are due to the Biological Education Committee for the invitation to prepare this booklet, and to the publishers for their assistance in its preparation. A number of people have read parts of the manuscript in draft and I am grateful for their helpful comments. In addition, I wish to thank my wife, Janet Ann, and Miss Lorraine Bonsor for help in preparing the illustrations; Mrs Janet Abrahams for the care and patience with which she has converted my hand-written scrawl into type; C. Atherton, Esq for Plate 2; and E. C. Hemken, Esq for taking the frontispiece which illustrates the theme of the booklet.

Henfield, Sussex   J.F.S.
1968

Contents

1 Plants and Water
   1.1   The importance of water to plants   1
   1.2   Effects of the availability of water on plant structure   2
   1.3   Transpiration   3
   1.4   Water content of plants   4

2 Structure and Physical Properties of Water
   2.1   The water molecule   6
   2.2   Dissociation of water   8
   2.3   Isotopes in water   8
   2.4   Physical properties of water   9

3 Movement of Water
   3.1   Mass flow   12
   3.2   Diffusion   13
   3.3   Osmosis   17
   3.4   Matric potential   20
   3.5   Electro-osmosis   20

4 Water Relations of Cells and Tissues
   4.1   The vacuolated plant cell   22
   4.2   Water relations of a vacuolated cell   23
   4.3   Plasmolysis   25
   4.4   Water relations of parenchyma   27
   4.5   Determination of the osmotic potential of vacuolar sap   28
   4.6   Measurement of water potential   31
   4.7   Non-osmotic water absorption   33

5 The Mechanism of Stomatal Movement
   5.1   Morphology of stomata   37
   5.2   Patterns of stomatal response   38
   5.3   Measurement of stomatal size   39
   5.4   Mechanism of stomatal opening and closure   42

6 Transpiration
   6.1   Measurement of transpiration   46
   6.2   Water consumption by crops and natural vegetation   51
   6.3   Environmental factors affecting transpiration   52
   6.4   Effects of plant structure on transpiration   53
   6.5   Diffusion through stomata   55
   6.6   Control of transpiration   57

7   Movement of Water through Plants
    7.1   Introduction   61
    7.2   Availability of soil water   62
    7.3   Movement of water into the stele   63
    7.4   Root pressure and guttation   66
    7.5   The pathway of water transport   67
    7.6   Velocity of flow   70
    7.7   Mechanisms of water movement   71

Further Reading   77

References   79

Plants and Water 1

1.1 The importance of water to plants

Without water, life as we know it could not exist. Living organisms originated in an aqueous environment and they have, in the course of evolution, become absolutely dependent on water in a variety of ways. It is essential to plants for the following reasons:

(1) It is a constituent of protoplasm, sometimes comprising as much as 95 per cent of the total weight. When protoplasm is dehydrated it ceases to be active and below a certain water content it is killed. This is because most of the organic substances in protoplasm, including carbohydrates, proteins and nucleic acids, are hydrated in their natural state, and if this water is removed, their physical and chemical properties are affected.

(2) Water participates directly in a number of chemical reactions occurring in protoplasm. Hydrolysis and condensation reactions, in which water is added to, or removed from organic molecules, are important in various metabolic processes, such as the interconversion of carbohydrates, e.g.

$$(C_6H_{10}O_5)_n + nH_2O \rightleftharpoons nC_6H_{12}O_6;$$

starch $\qquad\qquad$ glucose

and of organic acids, e.g.

$$HOOC.CH{=}CH.COOH + H_2O \rightleftharpoons HOOC.CH_2.CHOH.COOH.$$

fumaric acid $\qquad\qquad\qquad$ malic acid

It is a source of hydrogen atoms for the reduction of carbon dioxide in photosynthesis, and is a product of respiration.

(3) In addition, water is the solvent in which many other substances are dissolved, and in which they undergo chemical reactions.

(4) Much of the water in plants occurs in large vacuoles within the protoplasts (Fig. 4–1, p. 22), where it is largely responsible for maintaining the rigidity ('*turgidity*') of cells and hence of the plant as a whole.

(5) There is a thin layer of water surrounding each cell of a plant and this permeates the micro-spaces between solid material in the cell wall. These surface films, which are continuous from cell to cell and form a network throughout the plant, are important in the entry and movement of dissolved substances.

(6) Water fulfils a variety of additional functions in plants; for example, it provides a medium for the movement of dissolved substances in the xylem and phloem. It is the medium through which motile gametes effect fertilization, and it assists in various ways in the dissemination of spores, fruits and seeds. In submerged or partly submerged aquatic plants, external water provides some support because of the buoyancy of stems and leaves.

1.2   Effects of the availability of water on plant structure

The structure of a plant is profoundly affected by the amount of water in the external environment. Because of the relatively low solubility of oxygen in water, aquatic plants, termed *hydrophytes*, generally have less oxygen immediately available to them than have plants whose surfaces are exposed to air. The availability of oxygen is improved in some aquatic plants, e.g. the water crowfoot (*Ranunculus aquatilis*), by an increase in the surface area of submerged leaves and stems through the development of a filamentous habit. Oxygen can diffuse in readily over the whole plant surface; because the cuticle is thin. Stomata are usually absent or non-functional. There is an enormous development of intercellular spaces which serve to increase buoyancy as well as to facilitate gaseous diffusion from the aerial parts to submerged organs of the plant. Since they are capable of absorbing water and dissolved substances over a large part of their surface, many free-floating and some submerged plants, e.g. duckweeds (*Lemna* spp.), Canadian Pond-weed (*Elodea canadensis*) and horn-worts (*Ceratophyllum* spp.), have poorly developed root systems. In some aquatic plants, e.g. water-lilies, anchorage is secured by extensive rhizomes bearing adventitious roots. Specialized water-conducting cells are developed to a lesser extent in aquatic than in land plants and the mechanical supporting tissue is reduced. Such thick-walled cells as occur are concentrated towards the centre of the stem where they exert maximum effect in resisting the pull exerted by rapidly flowing water.

Hygrophytes, e.g. many mosses and liverworts and some ferns, are plants which inhabit damp situations where the air is humid and the soil is often saturated with water. Such habitats are generally shaded and hygrophytes commonly have a large surface area of leaves to facilitate photosynthesis. There is little control of water loss. Characteristically, hygrophytes can withstand temporary desiccation, becoming active again when water is supplied.

Mesophytes are plants which grow in well-aerated soils and have leaves exposed to moderately dry air. Most crop species and many of our native plants come into this category. They exert control of water loss mainly by regulating the size of the stomata.

Xerophytes are plants which are able to tolerate very dry conditions, at least temporarily. They usually have a well-developed root system which ensures an adequate supply of water from soils with a low water content. In addition, these plants exhibit features termed 'xeromorphic', which minimize water loss by evaporation. Characteristically these features include an impervious cuticle, a thick epidermis consisting of several layers of cells, sunken stomata, small intercellular spaces in the leaves, and reduction of leaf surface area. Sometimes the leaves are reduced to spines (e.g. in some cacti), and photosynthesis is restricted to the stem. *Phylloclades* are flattened, leaf-like branches which arise in the axils of reduced scale-like leaves in such plants as Butcher's Broom (*Ruscus aculeatus*). They are the main photosynthetic organs of these plants, and water loss from them is restricted by xeromorphic features.

Many xerophytes store water and this enables them to survive prolonged dry spells. Specialized water-storage tissues may occur in the stem (e.g. in many Cactaceae), in leaves (e.g. in *Sedum* spp., *Mesembryanthemum* spp.) or in roots (e.g. in some Umbelliferae and Compositae of desert regions). The water-storage organ in each case has a swollen appearance, and the plant is described as *succulent*. Another group of plants which exhibit succulence are the inhabitants of salt marshes (*halophytes*), e.g. saltworts (*Salicornia* spp.) but this may be an adaptation to reduce the concentration of absorbed sodium chloride within the plants and not for water storage as such.

1.3 Transpiration

Except in submerged aquatics, the amount of water retained by a plant is only a small fraction of the total absorbed by the roots. By far the greater part is transported to the aerial parts where it evaporates into the surrounding

Fig. 1-1 Relative amounts of water transpired (clear area), retained (shaded), and consumed (black) by maize (*Zea mays*) plants. (Data from MILLER, 1938)

air. The loss of water as vapour from plants is known as *transpiration*. It was estimated by MILLER that maize (*Zea mays*) plants transpire over 98 per cent of all the water they absorb. Most of the rest is retained in the plant and only a minute proportion (0·2 per cent) is used in photosynthesis (Fig. 1-1). These proportions are probably fairly representative for mesophytes growing under moderately dry conditions.

Transpiration has often been described as a 'necessary evil'. Exposure to the atmosphere of a large area of moist cell surfaces is necessary to facilitate the absorption of carbon dioxide and oxygen by leaves, and this inevitably causes loss of water by evaporation. If plants had evolved a cuticle which allowed the free passage of carbon dioxide and oxygen molecules, but not water, presumably they would not transpire. As has already been mentioned, some plants show adaptations which cause transpiration to be reduced, but this is only achieved at the expense of reduced carbon dioxide assimilation and slower growth. Closure of stomata at night, as commonly occurs (see Chapter 5), serves to conserve water at a time when photosynthesis is stopped by the absence of light.

It is likely that more plants die from lack of sufficient water to replace that lost in transpiration, than from any other single cause, and even a temporary water deficit can sometimes be fatal. In many parts of the world, including the British Isles, the yield of crops can be increased by artificial irrigation even in periods of normal rainfall. Spraying of crops with synthetic substances ('antitranspirants') which reduce the rate of evaporation of water from the leaves by causing partial closure of the stomata, is often effective in increasing yields, particularly in dry seasons.

From time to time it has been claimed that transpiration has some beneficial effects on plant growth which serve to mitigate the problems which its existence brings. It is possible that in some situations a plant may deplete the soil of inorganic nutrients in the immediate vicinity of its roots. This may occur to such an extent that growth is affected. A rapid rate of movement of water into a plant, as a result of transpiration, helps to prevent this by bringing dissolved substances to the root surface from more distant regions of the soil. There is some evidence that this effect may be important in the growth of agricultural crops. At one time it was believed that mineral salts were absorbed passively by roots and carried into the shoot via the transpiration stream. It now appears that absorption of water and dissolved substances at the root surface are largely independent processes and that once mineral salts enter the root cells adequate supplies are readily available to all parts of the plant, even at very low transpiration rates (see Chapter 7).

Leaves exposed to direct sunlight absorb a large amount of radiant energy, and in consequence there is a rise in temperature. Sometimes, heating is so severe that photosynthesis is inhibited for a time until the leaves cool down again. In such circumstances, the absorption of heat by water when it evaporates (see Chapter 2, p. 10) may be beneficial to the plant. However, it is doubtful whether the cooling effect of transpiration is of much significance except under extreme conditions.

1.4   Water content of plants

The water content of a plant, or its parts, can be determined in several ways. The usual method is to dry the material in an oven until it reaches constant weight. Care must be taken to avoid charring which is an indication of loss of dry matter, and for this reason a temperature of $80°C–100°C$ is commonly employed. A small amount of water associated with the organic material is not removed by this procedure.

Water content is usually expressed as a percentage of either fresh weight or dry weight. The former basis is in common use, but the latter is sometimes preferable especially when the water content is high, since, in this case, large variations in the amount of water present cause rather small changes when expressed on a percentage of fresh-weight basis. However, water content represented as a percentage of the dry weight can also be misleading because, if the dry weight changes, e.g. as a result of the production or consumption of storage products, water content per unit of dry weight will change even when the amount of water present remains constant. Table 1

Table 1   Water contents of various plants expressed as percentages of fresh weight (FW) and dry weight (DW)

Plant	Part	Water content as a percentage of:	
		FW	DW
lettuce (*Lactuca sativa*)	young leaves	94·3	1654
carrot (*Daucus carota*)	swollen root	90·3	931
strawberry (*Fragaria chiloensis*)	ripe fruit	89·1	817
lichen (*Peltigera canina*)	whole plant	77·2	339
runner bean (*Phaseolus coccineus*)	seed	20·3	25·5
barley (*Hordeum vulgare*)	grain	10·2	11·4
peanut (*Arachis hypogaea*)	seed	5·2	5·5

shows some typical water contents of various plant organs expressed on both fresh-weight and dry-weight bases. It must be emphasized that, especially in a growing plant, water content is an extremely variable quantity, changing rapidly with fluctuations in soil moisture and in the humidity of the air. This is particularly true of lichens and bryophytes in which there is a close correlation between water content and the relative humidity of the surrounding air.

Structure and Physical Properties of Water

2.1 The water molecule

When hydrogen and oxygen atoms combine to form water, electrons are shared between them in such a way that the resulting molecule is stable and unreactive (Fig. 2–1). Although the water molecule as a whole is electrically neutral, the asymmetric distribution of electrons results in one side being positively charged with respect to the other. Such molecules, which are termed '*dipoles*', tend to orientate themselves in an electrical field with the negative side towards the positive pole and vice versa.

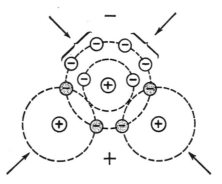

Fig. 2–1 Diagrammatic representation of the structure of a water molecule showing 'shared' (stippled) and 'lone pairs' (bracketed) of electrons, and the position of hydrogen bonds (arrowed).

Electrostatic attraction between the positively charged region of one molecule and the negatively charged region of a neighbouring one causes the formation of *hydrogen bonds*. These are rather weak forces having only about one twenty-fourth of the strength of a covalent O—H bond. Because of the presence of two protons (+) and two lone pairs of electrons (−), a water molecule can form up to four hydrogen bonds with surrounding molecules (Fig. 2–1). The bonds tend to be arranged tetrahedrally, and, because of this, the water molecules in ice form a regular tetrahedral crystalline structure. In liquid water the molecules are more irregularly arranged than in ice, and the hydrogen bonds linking them are more labile, but some crystallinity remains (Fig. 2–2). As the temperature rises, the extent of hydrogen bonding is reduced, but some is present even at boiling point. The chemical formula of

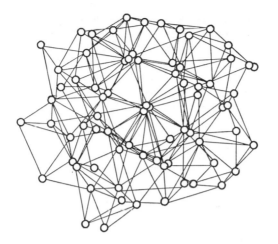

Fig. 2–2   Structural model of liquid water derived by computer analysis. (BERNAL, 1965)

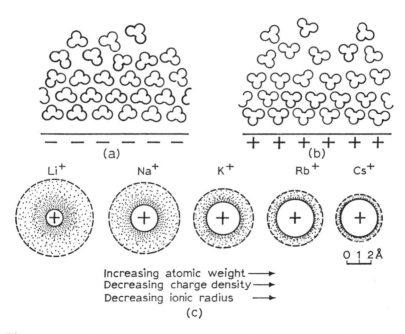

Fig. 2–3 (a), (b)   Orientation of water molecules at charged surfaces. **(c)** Relative sizes of hydrated alkali-metal cations. The stippled areas represent the shell of water molecules surrounding each ion.

water in the solid and liquid states, usually expressed as H_2O, is thus more correctly represented by $(H_2O)_n$, where n decreases as temperature rises.

Hydrogen bonds are also formed between water molecules and other charged particles or surfaces. At charged surfaces, layers of orientated water molecules are arranged as indicated in Fig. 2–3 (a), (b). The thickness of the layers depends on the intensity of the charges at the surfaces. When inorganic salts are dissolved in water they dissociate into negative and positive ions. Each ion is surrounded by a layer of orientated water molecules, and, in fact, it is because of the presence of these shells that ions remain separated in aqueous solution. The thickness of the hydration shell depends on the density of electrical charge on a particular ion, and is therefore greater for small ions than for larger ones carrying the same quantity of electrical charge (Fig. 2–3 (c)).

Water forms hydrogen bonds with organic molecules, especially with those containing carbonyl ($>C=O$), hydroxyl ($—OH$) and amino ($—NH_2$) groups. It is largely because of the presence of these groups that biologically important molecules such as proteins, carbohydrates and nucleic acids, have 'bound' water associated with them. BERNAL (1965) estimated that strongly orientated water molecules at the surface of some proteins may account for as much as 30 per cent of the weight of the hydrated molecule.

2.2   Dissociation of water

Water dissociates to a slight extent into hydronium ions and hydroxyl ions:

$$2H_2O \rightleftharpoons H_3O^+ + OH.^-$$

The hydrogen ion (H_3O^+) is a hydrated proton ($H^+ + H_2O$) and it is usually represented simply by H^+ and termed a hydrogen ion. The dissociation of water then becomes the familiar:

$$H_2O \rightleftharpoons H^+ + OH.^-$$

At equilibrium, the product of the concentrations of hydrogen ions and hydroxyl ions in pure water is constant, and has a value of about 10^{-14} gram-ions per litre (that is, one gram of hydrogen ions in 10^{14} litres of water.) Since the total number of hydrogen ions is exactly equal to the number of hydroxyl ions, each has a concentration of 10^{-7} gram-ions per litre. Pure water thus has a pH value of 7, since pH is defined as the negative logarithm of hydrogen ion concentration (pH $= -\log [H^+]$). The pH value of an aqueous solution is influenced by the presence of dissolved substances. Solutions in which the hydrogen ion concentration is greater than 10^{-7} gram-ions per litre (pH < 7) are acidic, whereas those in which the hydrogen ion concentration is lower than this (pH > 7) are alkaline.

2.3   Isotopes in water

So far it has been assumed that water consists solely of molecules containing ordinary hydrogen (^1H) and oxygen (^{16}O), with atomic weights of about 1 and 16 respectively. In fact, natural water also contains the hydrogen isotopes, deuterium (^{2}H) and tritium (^{3}H), and the oxygen isotopes, ^{17}O and ^{18}O. The amount of these isotopes present is relatively small; the ratio of ^{1}H to the next most abundant isotope, deuterium, being about 6500 to 1. Of the isotopes present in water molecules, only tritium is radioactive. It is formed in the atmosphere by the action of cosmic rays and has a half-life of 12·5 years.

2.4 Physical properties of water

Water is such a familiar substance that its unique physical properties are usually taken for granted. No one is surprised that water is a liquid at most ordinary temperatures, until its melting point and boiling point are compared with those of other substances of similar molecular size (Table 2).

Table 2 Some physical constants of water and other hydrides of low molecular weight

Substance	Chemical formula	Molecular weight	Melting point (°C)	Boiling point (°C)
methane	CH$_4$	16	−184	−161
ammonia	NH$_3$	17	−78	−33
WATER	H$_2$O	18	0	+100
hydrogen fluoride	HF	20	−92	+19
hydrogen sulphide	H$_2$S	34	−86	−61

From such a comparison, it appears that water has a much higher *melting point* and *boiling point* than might be expected. This is attributable to the association of water molecules with one another, causing the substance to behave as if it has a much higher molecular weight than the simple formula H$_2$O indicates (cf. p. 8). If this were not the case, water would be gaseous at normal temperatures and life as we know it on earth could not exist.

Water is also unusual in that its *specific heat* is the highest of any known substance. This means that it is relatively slow to heat up and cool down, a feature which is of considerable biological significance. The fundamental unit of heat, the gram calorie, is defined as the quantity of heat required to raise the temperature of one gram of water from 0°C to 1°C (Table 3).

The *latent heat of melting* and *heat of vaporization* are abnormally high also. The former is expressed as the number of calories required to convert one gram of solid at freezing point into liquid at the same temperature. The value of approximately 80 calories per gram indicates that about the same amount of heat is required to melt ice as to raise the temperature of the resulting liquid to 80°C. Heat of vaporization is similarly defined as the number of calories required to change one gram of liquid into vapour. Its magnitude depends on the temperature at which vaporization occurs, being lower at higher temperatures. The implication of these facts in relation to plants is that a relatively large amount of heat must be abstracted from water before it freezes, whereas evaporation has a strong cooling effect.

Table 3   Some physical constants of pure water

specific heat (cal/g)	1
latent heat of melting (cal/g)	80
heat of vaporization (cal/g)	588·9 (15°C)
saturation vapour pressure (mm Hg)	12·78 (15°C)
density (g/cm³)	0·99913 (15°C)
	1·00000 (4°C)
	0·99987 (0°C)
density of saturated vapour (g/cm³)	$12·85 \times 10^{-6}$
surface tension (dyn/cm)	73·4 (15°C)
viscosity (g/cm/sec)	$1·14 \times 10^{-2}$ (15°C)
tensile strength (mm Hg/cm²)	$10·64 \times 10^{-3}$
thermal conductivity (cal/cm/sec/°C)	$1·42 \times 10^{-3}$

Most liquids contract on cooling, reaching maximum density at freezing point, but water has a *maximum density* at 4°C (Table 3). For this reason water rarely freezes solid in the sea or in deep lakes, even in the coldest climates. When the temperature of the deeper water decreases below 4°C, the water rises as its density falls, and ice forms on the surface. This tends to prevent the water below from being cooled down to freezing point.

Water has the highest *surface tension* of all common liquids except mercury. It will rise by capillarity in a glass tube, 0·03 mm in diameter, to a height of almost 4 feet (120 cm). Consequently, water moves extensively by capillarity through narrow cavities in soil and in plant cell walls. The high *viscosity* and *tensile strength* of water (Table 3) are also significant in water movement through plants (see Chapter 7).

It should be noted that the physical properties of water are affected appreciably by the presence of dissolved substances. For further information about this, the article by KOHN (1965) may be consulted.

It is of considerable importance to plants that liquid water is almost colourless. The high transmission of visible light makes it possible for aquatic plants to photosynthesize when submerged at considerable depths, and for light to penetrate into deeply-seated tissues of leaves. Water absorbs light to some extent, particularly at the red end of the spectrum, and this accounts for the blue-green colour of light transmitted through a thick layer of water. There is strong absorption in the infra-red region which makes water a relatively good heat insulator, although its thermal conductivity is high (Table 3) compared with other liquids.

From the above account, it will appear that water is ideally suited for its functions in plants. This is true only because plants have evolved in such a way that they are able to exploit to greatest advantage the unique properties of water.

3.1 Mass flow

If two vessels, A and B, one containing water and the other empty, are connected by a pipe as shown in Fig. 3–1, water will flow from A into B when the tap (T) is opened, until its level in the two containers is the same. The rate of flow, dv/dt depends on the hydrostatic pressure gradient, ΔP, and on the resistance, R, offered by the connecting pipe, thus:

$$\frac{dv}{dt} = \frac{\Delta P}{R}$$

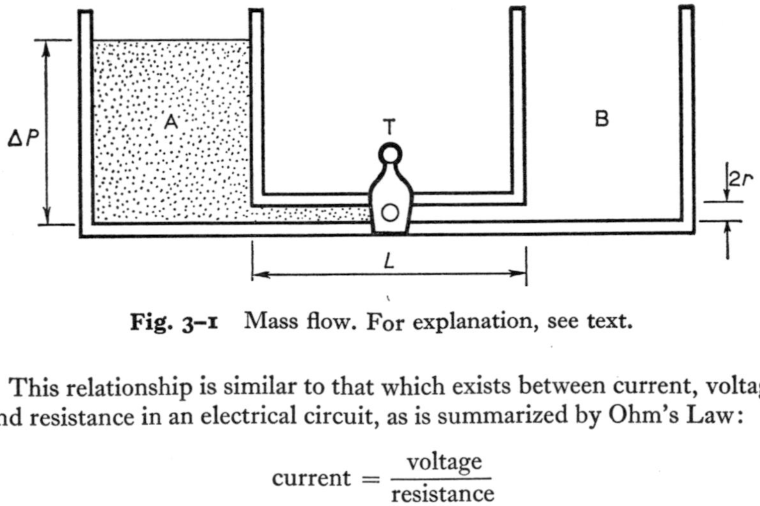

Fig. 3–1   Mass flow. For explanation, see text.

This relationship is similar to that which exists between current, voltage and resistance in an electrical circuit, as is summarized by Ohm's Law:

$$\text{current} = \frac{\text{voltage}}{\text{resistance}}$$

In the example illustrated, R depends on the length of the connecting pipe (L), its radius (r) and the viscosity of water (η = Gr. 'eta'). For relatively slow rates of flow:

$$R = \frac{8\eta L}{\pi r^4}$$

thus: $$\frac{dv}{dt} = \frac{\Delta P \pi r^4}{8\eta L} \quad \text{(Poiseuille's Law)}$$

As water flows from A into B, ΔP decreases until it becomes zero, and an equilibrium is established. Further movement of water from A to B could be brought about either by application of mechanical pressure to the water in A or by exerting a negative pressure (suction) to the liquid in B. In either case, the hydrostatic pressure of the water in A would be increased above that in B and water would flow along the hydrostatic pressure gradient that was created.

In *mass flow*, all the molecules present in the liquid, including those of dissolved substances, move simultaneously in the same direction.

3.2   Diffusion

In contrast to mass flow, *diffusion* involves the random spontaneous movement of individual molecules. Consider the evaporation of water from a beaker placed in an enclosed space at a uniform temperature. Until the air surrounding the vessel becomes saturated with water vapour, molecules of water in the liquid phase have a higher mean energy content ('chemical potential') than those in the gaseous phase, so that more of them acquire sufficient energy in a given time to escape into the air than are able to condense from the air into the liquid. However, when the air becomes saturated with water the movement of water molecules is equal in the two directions, and *net* diffusion stops. Thus, diffusion depends on a difference of chemical potential (sometimes expressed as vapour pressure) in much the same way as mass flow is caused by a difference in hydrostatic pressure. *Water potential* (ψ = Gr. 'psi') is a term which has been introduced to express the *difference* between the chemical potential of water at any point in a system (μ_w) and that of pure water under standard conditions (μ^0_w). Absolute values of chemical potential are not readily obtainable, but water potential can easily be determined because:

$$\psi = \mu_w - \mu^0_w = RT \ln (e/e^0)$$

where R is the ideal gas constant (erg/mole/degree); T, the absolute temperature (°K); e, the vapour pressure of water in the system at temperature T; and e^0 the vapour pressure of pure water at the same temperature. The units of $RT \ln e/e^0$ are erg/mole.* When e/e^0 is less than 1, as is usually the case in biological systems, $\ln e/e^0$ is negative and the water potential is expressed as a negative quantity. Water potential is increased by mechanical pressure or by an increase in temperature, and is lowered by the presence of dissolved solutes.

N.B. Water tends to diffuse from a region of higher to one of lower water potential (cf. transfer of heat from a region of higher to one of lower temperature). The more negative the water potential in a system, the greater the tendency for water to diffuse into it.

Chemical potentials are generally expressed in energy units (erg/mole) and water potential can also be expressed in the same units. It is usually

---

* The erg is equal to the work done when a force of 1 dyne acts through a distance of 1 cm; the dyne being the force which acting on a mass of 1 gram gives an acceleration of 1 cm per sec per sec.

more convenient however in discussing plant–water relations to use pressure units (atmospheres or bars). Energy units can be converted to pressure units by dividing by the partial molal volume of water V_w thus:

$$\frac{\mu_w - \mu^0_w}{V_w} = \frac{RT \ln (e/e^0)}{V_w}$$

The units of this equation are:

$$\frac{erg/mole}{cm^3/mole} = \frac{erg}{cm^3} = dyne/cm^2$$

$$1 \text{ bar} = 0.987 \text{ atm} = 10^6 \text{ dynes/cm}^2$$

If an aqueous solution is placed in an enclosed space the water content of the air at equilibrium is *lower* than when equilibrium is established with pure water. This fact is made use of when it is desired to maintain air in a closed container at different relative humidities (Table 4). If two vessels, one containing pure water and the other an aqueous solution, are placed in a closed atmosphere, water will gradually diffuse from the water into the solution along the existing gradient of water potential, i.e. from the region of higher to that of lower water potential.

Table 4   The relative humidities (RH)* of air in equilibrium with various concentrations of sodium chloride and sulphuric acid at 20°C

NaCl (M)	0.1	0.2	0.4	0.6	0.8	1.0	2.0	3.0	4.0	5.0
RH (%)	99.7	99.4	98.8	98.1	97.5	96.8	93.0	88.3	83.0	78.4
H_2SO_4 (specific gravity)	1.125	1.19	1.25	1.293	1.33	1.38	1.41	1.486	1.58	
RH (%)	90	80	70	60	50	40	30	20	10	

* RH is the ratio of the equilibrium vapour pressure in presence of the solution to the saturation vapour pressure over pure water at the same temperature.

The rate of diffusion of substances whether it be through air or in solution can be calculated from Fick's law

$$\frac{dn}{dt} = -Da \frac{dc}{dx}$$

where dn is the quantity of the substance which passes in time, dt, across an area a, and dc is the difference of chemical potential over a distance dx. In the case of diffusion of water, dc/dx can be represented by the gradient of water potential $\Delta\psi/dx$. D is a *diffusion coefficient* which varies for different substances and is affected to some extent by temperature and concentration (Table 5). The negative sign preceding it in the equation takes account of the fact that *net diffusion occurs from a region of higher to one of lower chemical potential.*

Table 5 Diffusion coefficients of certain substances in water. (From KOHN 1965)

Substance	Temp. (°C)	Conc.	$D(cm^2/sec) \times 10^5$
CO_2	20	—	1·7
O_2	25	—	2·92
NaCl	25	0·001 M	1·585
KCl	20	0·001 M	1·739
KCl	25	0·001 M	1·964
KNO_3	25	0·001 M	1·899
Glucose	25	0·39 %	0·673
Sucrose	25	0·38 %	0·521
H_2O	20	—	1·85
H_2O	25	—	2·13

Diffusion in liquids and solids, unlike diffusion in gases, is a discontinuous process in which at one time a molecule is moving rapidly from one point to another in the solvent and at another time merely vibrating or rotating about a mean position. The molecule is restrained in this position by the forces of attraction between it and neighbouring molecules which act as a potential energy barrier. When it acquires sufficient kinetic energy (activation energy) to overcome the barrier it becomes free to diffuse until it loses its kinetic energy by molecular collision, or in some other way.

When the potential energy barrier is comparatively low as in the diffusion of small molecules in water at physiological temperatures, the *activation energy* of diffusion is low and the temperature coefficient (Q_{10}*) of the process is small ($\simeq$ 1·2–1·3). On the other hand, when the potential energy barrier is high, as for example for diffusion through a viscous fluid or across a membrane, the activation energy of diffusion is higher and the process has a correspondingly high Q_{10}.

The permeability of a membrane, that is the ease with which a particular substance diffuses across it, may be represented by a permeability coefficient K (cf. diffusion coefficient D). K for water, sometimes termed '*hydraulic conductivity*', is commonly expressed as the distance moved by molecules in unit time for a given gradient of water potential. It is not yet possible to measure the permeability coefficient of single membranes in plant cells, but attempts have been made to determine K for the layer of cytoplasm separating the vacuole from the external solution (see Fig. 4–1, p. 22). One way

* Q_{10} is defined as the ratio of the rate of a process at a particular temperature to its rate at a temperature 10°C lower.

Table 6   Water permeability of plant cells

Plant species	Type of cell	K (μ/atm/hr)	Investigator
Salvinia auriculata	plasmolysed	3–33	HUBER and HÖFLER (1930)
Fucus	egg	8–22	RESÜHR (1935)
Tolypellopsis sp.		65	PULVA (1939)
Allium cepa	epidermal	18–66	DE HAAN (1933)
	isolated protoplast	21	LEVITT, SCARTH and GIBBS (1936)
Beta vulgaris	unplasmolysed	0·7	MYERS (1951)
	plasmolysed	13	MYERS (1951)
Nitella flexilis		420–1110	KAMIYA and TAZAWA (1956)
Chara australis		336	DAINTY and GINZBURG (1964)

of doing this is to make water flow in at one end of a long plant cell and out at the other by applying a gradient of water potential between the two ends (the method of *transcellular osmosis*). Giant cells of *Nitella* spp. and *Chara* spp. have been used successfully for such investigations. Another method is to measure the rate of uptake or loss of water by cells placed in solutions of different osmotic potentials (see below). Some experimentally determined values for water permeability of various types of cells are presented in Table 6.

A biological membrane is believed to consist basically of a bimolecular

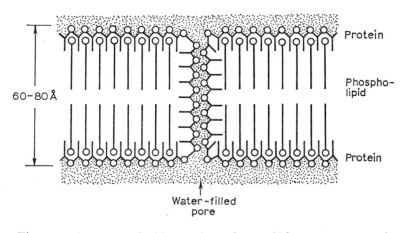

Fig. 3–2   Structure of a biological membrane. (After DANIELLI, 1954)

layer of oriented phospho-lipid molecules coated on each surface with a layer of protein (Fig. 3–2). It is thought that water penetrates the membrane through minute pores which are too small to allow dissolved substances to pass through easily. This is possible despite the association of water molecules with one another, because they readily become oriented into files of sufficiently small dimensions. The resistance of membranes to diffusion of solutes is thus many times greater than it is to water (see below).

Special mechanisms requiring metabolic energy exist to transport ions and organic molecules into cells, where they are retained by the low permeability of the membranes.

3·3   Osmosis

When an aqueous solution, for example of sucrose, is separated from pure water by a membrane which is more permeable to water than it is to the solute (a so-called 'semi-permeable membrane', SPM) more water molecules diffuse in a given time from the pure solvent into the solution than in the reverse direction, in response to the existing gradient of water potential. Such movement, known as '*osmosis*', can be demonstrated in an apparatus such as that shown in Fig. 3–3. Although it is generally applied to systems

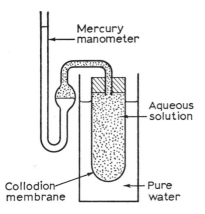

Fig. 3–3   A simple osmometer. For explanation, see text.

in which there is net movement of water, the word 'osmosis' may strictly be applied to the diffusion of *any* substance across a differentially permeable membrane in response to a gradient of chemical potential.

The movement of water across the membrane of an osmometer can be reduced by application of mechanical pressure to the solution which raises the potential of water in the solution and thus reduces the water potential gradient. When a state of equilibrium is established in this way in an osmometer with pure water outside a membrane, which is effectively impermeable to the solute, the excess pressure applied to the solution is termed its osmotic pressure.

Thus, the osmotic pressure of a solution may be defined as the excess hydrostatic pressure which must be applied to it in order to make its water potential equal to that of pure water. Since no actual pressure is developed unless the solution is placed in an osmometer it is preferable to use the term 'osmotic potential' instead of osmotic pressure. Osmotic potential, by convention designed Π (Gr. 'pi'), is given a negative sign, and it is then equal to the water potential of a solution at atmospheric pressure.

The great German plant physiologist, PFEFFER (1877), demonstrated that the osmotic potential developed by dilute aqueous solutions of sucrose is directly proportional to the concentration of solute and the absolute temperature. His observations enabled the Dutch chemist, VAN'T HOFF, to formulate a kinetic theory for dilute solutions and to show the applicability of the gas-law equation

$$PV = RT$$

Thus :

$$\text{osmotic potential} = -\frac{n}{V}.RT$$

where n is the number of molecules of solute in V litres of solution; R, the gas constant; and T, the absolute temperature.

The osmotic potential of a solution at extreme dilution is thus numerically equal to the pressure that the solute molecules would exert if they were in gaseous form occupying a volume equal to the volume of the solution. This led to the conclusion, by analogy with the behaviour of molecules in a gas, that osmotic potential is in some way produced by bombardment of solute molecules against the semi-permeable membrane. This view fails to take account of the fact that the component of the solution which moves is the solvent, and modern interpretations of osmotic potential invoke the influence of solute in effectively diluting the water and hence lowering of its potential.

On the basis of the Van't Hoff equation a molar solution of a non-electrolyte, such as sucrose, should have an osmotic potential of −22·4 atm (−22·7 bars) at N.T.P. In fact, experimentally determined values are appreciably lower than the theoretical (Table 7). This is attributed to various causes, including association between solvent molecules, hydration of solute, and to the fact that a litre of a solution contains less than 1000 grams of water because of the volume occupied by solute.

The osmotic potential of an aqueous solution of an electrolyte is lower (i.e. more negative) than that of a non-electrolyte at equi-molar concentration because an electrolyte in aqueous solution is dissociated into ions, and osmotic potential is proportional to the total concentration of particles, whether molecules or ions, in the solution. It was from the apparently

Table 7   Osmotic potentials (atmospheres) of solutions of given molal* and molar† concentration at 20°C

Conc.	Molal Sucrose	Molar Sucrose	Molar KCl	Molar NaCl
0·1	−2·6	−2·64	−4·6	−4·3
0·2	−5·1	−5·29	−8·8	−8·4
0·3	−7·6	−8·13	−12·6	−12·5
0·4	−10·1	−11·1	−16·7	−16·6
0·5	−12·8	−14·3	−20·6	−21·0
0·6	−15·4	−17·8	−24·1	−25·7
0·7	−18·1	−21·5	−28·3	−29·7
0·8	−20·9	−25·5	−32·2	−34·2
0·9	−23·7	−29·7	−35·9	−38·6
1·0	−26·6	−34·6	−39·2	−43·2

* A molal solution is 1 gram molecular weight + 1000 grams of water.
† A molar solution contains 1 gram molecular weight in 1 litre of solution.

anomalous values of osmotic potential observed with salt solutions that Arrhenius was led to propose the ionic theory of solution.

If two aqueous solutions have the same osmotic potential they are said to be *iso-osmotic* irrespective of the solute and its concentration. A solution which has a higher osmotic potential (i.e. lower osmotic pressure) than another is said to be *hypo-osmotic* with respect to the other (*hyper-osmotic*) solution. The terms 'isotonic', 'hypotonic' and 'hypertonic' are sometimes used synonomously with the above, but their use is better restricted to biological systems (see below, p. 25).

The osmotic potential of an aqueous solution can be determined experimentally in several ways. One of the most accurate methods is to measure the freezing point of a solution. The depression of the freezing point (ΔT) is related to osmotic potential (Π)—thus:

$$\Pi = -12 \cdot 04 \, \Delta T$$

Methods have been devised for determining osmotic potential thermo-electrically, by measuring the temperature of drops of solution from which water is evaporating under standard conditions. The apparatus is calibrated with solutions of known osmotic potential (BALDES and JOHNSON, 1939; SPANNER, 1951).

The osmotic potential of a solution can be estimated approximately by comparison with solutions of known osmotic potential using *Barger's method*. Small drops of the solution to be examined and of solutions of a range of known osmotic potentials are placed alternately in a capillary tube of about 1 mm internal diameter. If the inner surface of the tube is first coated with a layer of liquid silicone, the drops remain discrete and their lengths can be accurately measured with the aid of a travelling microscope. Water tends to diffuse from a drop of solution having a higher osmotic potential to one having a lower (see p. 13). When a pair of solutions are found which in the drops do not change in size over a period of time, it is concluded that these solutions have the same osmotic potential.

3.4   Matric potential

So far the effects on water potential of two factors, hydrostatic pressure and the presence of solute, have been discussed. A third factor which is important in determining the chemical potential of water in soil and in biological systems is the attraction between water molecules and the matrix (e.g. soil particles, cell walls or organic molecules) with which they are in contact (see p. 8). To these forces the term matric potential or 'imbibition pressure' (τ = Gr. 'tau') is applied. Matric potential is the cause of the swelling of such substances as gelatine and cellulose in water and is responsible for the initial swelling of soaked seeds. Considerable pressures are exerted by a swelling imbibant if it is confined in some way. It has been estimated that air-dry pea seeds when soaked in water may develop pressures as high as 1000 atm.

Water diffuses into an imbibing matrix along a gradient of water potential caused by a lowering of the chemical potential of the water at the imbibing surfaces. As more water is absorbed its potential there increases towards zero (i.e. it becomes less negative) and an equilibrium is eventually attained when the potentials of water in the matrix and bathing solution are the same. To extract water from the system it is necessary to lower the potential of water in the solution, e.g. by addition of a solute. The relationship between the osmotic potential of the solution and the amount of water withdrawn is not, however, a simple one because the first molecules of water adsorbed by a matrix are held by much greater forces than hold those imbibed subsequently. Therefore, it is possible to remove an appreciable amount of water from a water-saturated imbibant by decreasing the osmotic potential of the external solution by a few atmospheres, but at higher concentration of solution a decrease of several hundred atmospheres may be necessary to remove the same amount of water.

3.5   Electro-osmosis

When an electrical potential gradient is established in a solution containing charged solute particles there is a migration of the particles through the solvent to the anode or cathode according to their charge. This process is called 'electrophoresis' and is made use of, for example, in the separation of proteins. If, on the other hand, the charged particles are fixed, e.g. on the surface of the pores in a membrane (Fig. 3–4) then an electrical potential gradient causes movement of solvent. Such movement is known as electro-

osmosis. Negative charges in the wall of a pore induce positive charges in the surface layers of water molecules within the pore and the charged water then moves in the direction of the negative pole in response to an electrochemical potential gradient. Conversely, positively charged pore surfaces induce negative charges in the water layer and cause movement in the reverse direction.

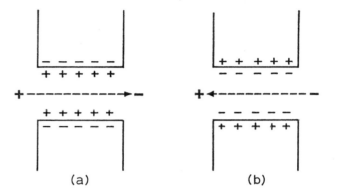

Fig. 3–4   *Electro-osmosis*. The arrows indicate the direction of flow of water when the pores of the membrane are charged; (a) −vely; and (b) +vely.

Water Relations of Cells and Tissues 4

4.1 The vacuolated plant cell

The structure of a typical vacuolated plant cell is represented diagrammatically in Fig. 4–1(a). The *cell wall*, consisting largely of cellulose, is a

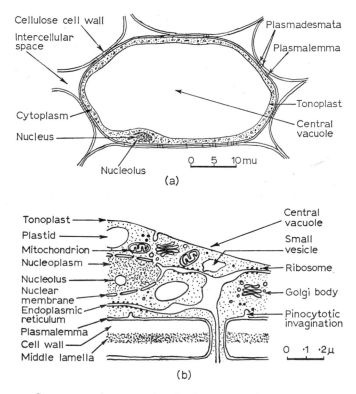

Fig. 4–1 Structure of a vacuolated plant cell. (a) Low magnification. (b) Electron-microscopic structure.

relatively rigid structure but it has some elasticity and so is capable of being stretched. Except when it is impregnated with fatty materials, as for example in cork cells, the cellulose wall is highly permeable to both water and dissolved substances. Characteristically, the *cytoplasm* forms a thin layer lining the inner surface of the cell wall from which it is separated by a lipo-protein membrane—the *plasmalemma*. Most of the volume of the cell is taken up by a large *vacuole* which is filled with an aqueous solution of inorganic and organic substances. The concentration of these substances is such that vacuolar sap commonly has an osmotic potential in the range of − 5 to − 30 atmospheres. The vacuole is bounded by a membrane, the *vacuolar membrane*, or *tonoplast*, which in structure closely resembles the plasmalemma. The internal structure of cytoplasm is complex as Fig. 4–1(b) indicates. There is an internal system of membranes, the *endoplasmic reticulum*, which effectively divides the cytoplasm into two phases, one of which is homogeneous and contains an aqueous solution which some people believe to be continuous with the external medium, and the other contains a variety of organelles, including mitochondria, plastids, golgi bodies, ribosomes and small isolated vacuoles. The cytoplasm of one cell is continuous with that of its neighbours through protoplasmic connections or *plasmadesmata*, and the whole cytoplasmic system in a plant is called the *symplast*.

4.2　Water relations of a vacuolated cell

The cytoplasm in an individual cell behaves as a semi-permeable membrane, separating the vacuole from the external solution bathing the cell wall. Because the volume of cytoplasm is relatively small compared with that of the vacuole it is customary to treat the water relations of vacuolated cells as if the cytoplasm was a membrane of negligible thickness. This is obviously an over-simplification as cytoplasmic volume is often an appreciable fraction of the total cell volume, and, furthermore, it does not remain constant under different conditions. As vacuolar volume alters with changes in the water potential of the medium, so also does cytoplasmic volume.

The idea that a vacuolated plant cell behaves as an osmometer emerged during the latter part of the nineteenth century, mainly through the work of PFEFFER and a Dutch botanist, HUGO DE VRIES. At first, only the difference in osmotic potential (OP) between vacuolar sap and external medium was considered to be important, but later it became clear that the mechanical pressure exerted by the stretched cell wall on the vacuolar sap must be taken into consideration. This *wall pressure* causes an equal and opposite counter pressure in accordance with Newton's third law of motion, and this is called *turgor pressure*. The terms 'turgor pressure' (TP) and 'wall pressure' (WP) are often used synonymously because they are equal in magnitude, but it is important to appreciate that they are exerted in opposite directions. The cause of water entering the vacuole (called by the early workers 'suction force' or 'suction pressure') was seen to be the resultant of two forces, namely, a difference of osmotic potential (or osmotic pressure as it was then called) between the vacuolar sap and external solution which tends to cause water to enter the cell, and the mechanical pressure exerted by the wall which tends to force water out.

In 1945, the American botanist B. S. MEYER proposed the term 'Diffusion Pressure Deficit' (DPD) to replace suction pressure. The DPD of water in a system (e.g. vacuolar sap) was defined as the amount in atmospheres by which the diffusion pressure of water in it is less than the diffusion pressure of pure water at the same temperature and pressure. This terminology attained wide-spread usage in the United States and has gradually been accepted elsewhere. Nowadays, however, the term 'diffusion pressure' is rarely used in the physical sciences, having been replaced by terms such as 'chemical potential' or 'chemical activity'. Water potential expresses the same property of a system as DPD, and in fact the two are numerically equal, although they are opposite in sign, i.e.

$$\psi = -\mathrm{DPD}$$

There is no justification for continued use of the term DPD and in what follows the thermodynamic terminology of water potential and water potential difference will be employed.

The water potential of a plant cell (ψ_v) under isothermal conditions is determined by the concentration of solutes in the vacuole (i.e. its osmotic potential), the amount of water-binding substances ('matrix') and the pressure exerted by the cell wall, in accordance with the equation

$$\psi_v = \psi_s + \psi_m + \psi_t$$

where ψ_s, ψ_m and ψ_t represent the contributions made by solutes, matrix and turgor pressure respectively.

ψ_s and ψ_m are negative quantities while ψ_t is generally positive. ψ_m is often assumed to be negligible and the equation reduces to:

$$\psi_v = \psi_s + \psi_t$$

cf. $$-\mathrm{DPD} = -\mathrm{OP} + \mathrm{TP}$$
or $$\mathrm{DPD} = \mathrm{OP} - \mathrm{TP}$$

Water is taken up by a cell as long as ψ_v is lower (i.e. more negative) than the potential of the water in the bathing solution (ψ_e). Uptake of water dilutes the vacuolar sap and causes an increase in the value of ψ_s (i.e. it becomes less negative) and at the same time, because the cell swells, ψ_t also increases (becomes more positive). Thus, the value of ψ_v increases until it becomes equal to ψ_e at which point the uptake of water stops. If the bathing solution is pure water $(\psi_e = 0)$, then at equilibrium $\psi_v = 0$ and the cell is said to be *fully turgid*. Under such conditions

$$\psi_s = -\psi_t$$

or

$$\mathrm{OP} = \mathrm{TP}$$

On the other hand, if the external solution contains solutes (i.e. $\psi_e < 0$) equilibrium is established at less than maximum cell volume, i.e. when the cell is not fully turgid. At this point

$$\psi_s - \psi_e = -\psi_t.$$

A solution in which a cell retains exactly the same volume as *in vivo* is said to be isotonic. A hypertonic solution is one in which a cell shrinks and a hypotonic solution is one in which it swells (cf. 19.)

Figure 4–2 illustrates diagrammatically the changes which occurred in ψ_v, ψ_s and ψ_t when a plant cell was allowed to swell or shrink by being placed in solutions of various osmotic potentials. The values of ψ_v were obtained by observing the changes in volume when a cell was placed in a series of sucrose solutions of known osmotic potentials. ψ_s was calculated at each point from the cell volume assuming that the amount of solute in the vacuole remained

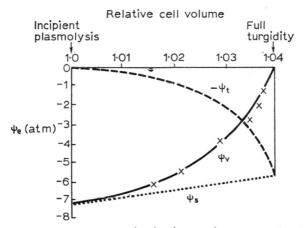

Fig. 4–2 Relationship between ψ_e, ψ_s, ψ_v and ψ_t in a vacuolated plant cell of *Nitella* sp. (Data of TAMIYA, 1938.) Note that ψ_s and ψ_v become less negative as the cell gets more turgid while ψ_t becomes *more* positive ($-\psi_t$, more negative). For further explanation, see text.

the same and ψ_t was estimated by difference. In the particular cell used, the cell volume at full turgidity was 4 per cent larger than in the solution at which ψ_t was just reduced to zero. The extent of the volume change observed in different cells depends on the degree of elasticity of the wall. In cells with very extensive cell walls, e.g. guard cells (see p. 38) a variation in volume of up to 25 per cent has been observed. It is worth noting that in *Nitella* cells the wall pressure curve is concave to the horizontal axis; this means that as the cell enlarges, a given change in ψ_e produces a progressively smaller increase in cell volume.

4.3 Plasmolysis

If a cell is placed in a solution of such low water potential that equilibrium is not attained by the time ψ_t falls to zero, water continues to be withdrawn from the cell along the existing gradient of potential. At first, the cell

wall may cave in slightly through adhesion to the cytoplasm with development of a small negative turgor pressure, but when the rigidity of the wall
prevents further distortion, the wall and protoplast begin to part company
('*incipient plasmolysis*') and the cell then becomes *plasmolysed* (Plate 2).
The vacuole continues to contract by loss of water until the potential of water
inside is equal to that of the external solution. At this point, the osmotic
potentials of the cell sap and external solution are approximately the same
although the former is somewhat lower (i.e. more negative) because of a
small hydrostatic pressure exerted by the surrounding cytoplasm ('cytoplasmic pressure'). This pressure has never been accurately measured in
plant cells, but red blood cells are said to have a cytoplasmic pressure equivalent to about 2 mm of water (0·003 atm).

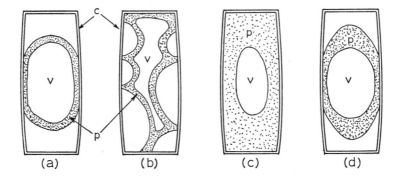

Fig. 4-3   Types of plasmolysis (a) convex, (b) concave, (c) tonoplast,
(d) cap. c = cell wall; p = protoplasm; v = vacuole.

On plasmolysis, the cytoplasm may assume a variety of forms, some of
which are shown in Fig. 4–3. *Convex plasmolysis* (Fig. 4–3(a)) occurs generally in mature cells and seems to be associated with a relatively low
cytoplasmic viscosity. In *concave* plasmolysis (Fig. 4–3(b)), which tends to
occur when cytoplasmic viscosity is high, the cytoplasm remains associated
with the cell wall at some points, probably in the region of plasmodesmata.
Cells which initially show concave plasmolysis often alter to the convex
form when plasmolysis is prolonged. In concave plasmolysis fine strands of
cytoplasm (strands of Hecht) can sometimes be seen connecting the rounded
cytoplasm to the wall.

The fact that the cytoplasm breaks away from the wall upon plasmolysis
shows that while the cell wall allows free passage of water and solutes, the
layer of cytoplasm behaves as a differentially permeable membrane. Semi-
permeability properties are associated with the plasmalemma and tonoplast,
and with the intervening membrane system in the bulk of the cytoplasm. If
only the plasmalemma were involved, the volume of the cytoplasmic layer

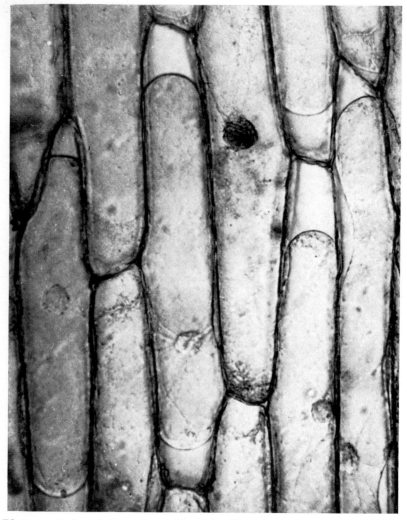

Plate 2 Onion bulb scale epidermal cells mounted in 0·5 M sucrose solution. Note that some, but not all, of the cells are plasmolysed.

would decrease on plasmolysis to the same extent as does the cell vacuole. On the other hand, if the tonoplast were the sole functional membrane, the vacuole would contract and the volume of the cytoplasm would increase correspondingly. Unfortunately it is not yet possible to make sufficiently accurate measurements to estimate the extent to which cytoplasmic volume alters on plasmolysis and it is generally assumed that it decreases with decrease in vacuolar volume. However, in tonoplast plasmolysis (Fig. 4–8(c)), which can be induced by treatment of cells with solutions containing potassium thiocyanate, the vacuole decreases in volume while the cytoplasmic volume increases. This treatment has apparently destroyed the semi-permeability properties of the plasmalemma. Unlike convex and concave plasmolysis, tonoplast plasmolysis cannot be reversed, presumably because the cytoplasm has been irreversibly injured. Cap plasmolysis is an intermediate condition sometimes observed in which the cytoplasm swells at the ends of the cell (Fig. 4–3(d)).

Normally, plasmolysed cells remain alive for an indefinite period, and if deplasmolysed slowly they may return to normal condition without injury. When kept in the plasmolysing solution for a long time they gradually deplasmolyse, because accumulation of solutes from the external medium lowers the osmotic potential of the vacuolar sap and maintains a gradient of water potential. This phenomenon illustrates a property of the cytoplasmic layer which distinguishes it from a non-living semi-permeable membrane. Although cytoplasm has a high resistance to the passive penetration of many solutes, ions and organic molecules are transferred across it unidirectionally even against an existing electro-chemical potential gradient, albeit at a slow rate relative to the rate of movement of water (see p. 17).

While plasmolysis is an interesting phenomenon illustrating some of the properties of plant cells, it does not normally occur in nature. The cells of plant roots adapted to grow in solutions of low osmotic potential, e.g. in sea water, have a correspondingly highly concentrated vacuolar sap. An extreme value of -202 atm was recorded for the osmotic potential of vacuolar sap extracted from a species of *Atriplex* growing on the shores of Salt Lake in Utah. Cells, e.g. in a wilting leaf, which are losing water by evaporation faster than they can replace it do not usually become plasmolysed, but in extreme cases the cell contents become disorganized and the cell walls may collapse. This phenomenon is termed '*cytorrhysis*'.

4.4   Water relations of parenchyma

Individual cells in a tissue are subjected to pressures and tensions imposed on them by surrounding cells, and for this reason the water potential of a cell after it has been isolated from a plant is usually different from that of the same cell in the intact organism. If a given cell is subjected to compression by those surrounding it, its turgor pressure will be effectively increased and its water potential correspondingly reduced. Conversely, tensions may be established which tend to stretch the cell wall causing turgor pressure to be reduced, and in extreme cases ψ_t may become negative.

All the cells in a tissue at equilibrium have the same water potential because those which tend to develop a more negative potential withdraw

Table 8 Approximate values of ψ_s and ψ_t (in atmospheres) when cells having differing concentrations of vacuolar sap come to equilibrium with a solution having an osmotic potential of -10 atmospheres

The values of ψ_s are calculated from the estimated volumes of vacuole (V) in the cells at the different states of turgidity. V is expressed as a percentage of its value when the cell is in pure water. The gas-law relationship is assumed to hold and cytoplasmic pressure and matric potential are assumed to be negligible.

ψ_e Atm		Cells		
		A	B	C
0	ψ_s	-5	-10	-15
	ψ_t	5	10	15
	V	100	100	100
-10	ψ_s	-10	$-11 \cdot 8$	$-16 \cdot 9$
	ψ_t	0	$1 \cdot 8$	$6 \cdot 9$
	V	50*	85	89

* Cell plasmolysed.

water from surrounding cells in which the potential is higher. However, it should be clearly understood that the osmotic potentials of the sap in individual cells of such a tissue may be widely different. Cells with low osmotic potentials will have a correspondingly higher turgor pressure at equilibrium than will those in which the osmotic potential is higher (Table 8).

4.5 Determination of the osmotic potential of vacuolar sap

(a) Methods involving sap extraction

Uncontaminated sap can be extracted from the vacuoles of certain giant algal coenocytes, e.g. *Valonia* spp. with the aid of a micropipette. Fairly pure vacuolar sap can be obtained from large cells of the freshwater algae, *Nitella* spp., simply by cutting across a filament towards one end of a cell and squeezing the liquid out on to a slide with the aid of a glass rod.

The extraction of unaltered vacuolar sap from cells of higher plants presents much greater difficulty. A liquid can be squeezed from tissues in a suitably designed press, but its composition varies greatly depending upon the procedure adopted and the pressures applied. The liquid which comes out initially upon application of a few atmospheres pressure is mainly from the cell walls. As the pressure is increased, fractions containing vacuolar sap are obtained but these may be contaminated with material from the cytoplasm. There is also a possibility that the vacuolar sap may be diluted during extraction by filtration as it is squeezed out through the cytoplasm. This effect can be reduced by first freezing and then thawing the tissue before pressing. Unfortunately, this procedure increases the risk of contaminating the sap with cytoplasmic material.

The osmotic potential of an extracted liquid can be determined with considerable accuracy either by cryoscopy or by a vapour pressure determination (see Chapter 3, p. 19). SHIMSHI and LIVNE (1967) have devised a method of estimating the osmotic potential of plant cell sap from measurements of refractive index and electrical conductivity. Portable equipment, suitable for use in the field, is described.

(b) The method of limiting plasmolysis

This method is based on the assumption that at incipient plasmolysis the osmotic potential of cell sap is equal to that of the external medium, i.e. that turgor pressure is zero and that cytoplasmic pressure and matric potential are small enough to be ignored (Fig. 4–2). Since it is difficult to judge accurately the point of incipient plasmolysis in individual cells, the method is useful mainly to estimate the mean osmotic potential of the sap in a population of cells in a homogeneous tissue. Samples of the tissue (slices of a storage organ such as red beet root, cut 0·5 mm or less in thickness, and onion epidermis strips, work very well) are placed in solutions of known osmotic potential and allowed to reach equilibrium. This takes about 30

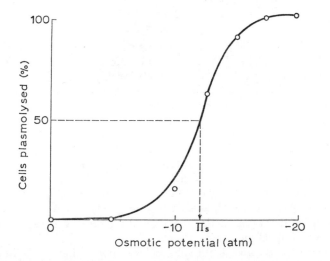

Fig. 4–4 Determination of the mean osmotic potential of vacuolar sap (Π_s) by the method of limiting plasmolysis. For explanation, see text.

minutes. They are then examined with a microscope and the percentage of cells visibly plasmolysed in each solution is recorded. The results can be plotted in the form of a graph and the osmotic potential corresponding to 50 per cent plasmolysis is taken to equal the mean value of the vacuolar sap (Π_s) at incipient plasmolysis (Fig. 4–4). In order to relate the value obtained to the osmotic potential of the sap in the fully turgid cell, it is necessary to make a correction for the difference in volume of the vacuole in the two conditions.

If Π_{ip} is the osmotic potential of the sap at incipient plasmolysis and V_{ip} is the volume of the vacuole at this point, then assuming that the VAN'T HOFF relationship (p. 18) holds:

$$\Pi_t = \Pi_{ip} \times \frac{V_{ip}}{V_t}$$

where Π_t and V_t are respectively the osmotic potential and volume of the sap in the turgid cell. V_{ip}/V_t can be estimated approximately from the ratio of the weights or volumes of the tissue in the solution which caused incipient plasmolysis and in pure water and Π_t can thus be calculated if Π_{ip} is known. For red beet tissue V_{ip}/V_t is approximately 0·95.

(c) The plasmometric method

This method, devised by HÖFLER, is applicable to individual cells. It involves determination of the volume of the cell vacuole initially (V_t), and after plasmolysis (V_p), in a solution of known osmotic potential, Π_p. The osmotic potential of the original sap Π_t is then calculated from the formula

$$\Pi_t = \Pi_p \times \frac{V_p}{V_t}$$

assuming that at equilibrium the osmotic potential of the sap in the plasmolysed cell is equal to Π_p; that is, cytoplasmic pressure and matric potential are negligible, and the VAN'T HOFF relationship holds.

This method can only be applied with reasonable accuracy to cells of regular shapes, e.g. spheres, cubes or cylinders, and when the plasmolysed protoplast assumes a regular form so that its vacuolar volume can be calculated from measurement of linear dimensions under the microscope. It is sometimes possible, e.g. in some epidermal cells of onion bulb scales (Plate 2), to treat the cell as a cylinder and the plasmolysed protoplast as a cylinder with hemispherical ends. The volume of the vacuole in the turgid cell (V_t) is then given by the formula $V_t = \pi r_t^2\, l_t$ and that of the plasmolysed vacuole by the formula $V_p = \pi r_p^2\, (l_p - \frac{2}{3} r_p)$; where $\pi \approx 3\cdot14$; l_p and l_t, the lengths of the vacuole in the plasmolysed and turgid cell respectively and r_p, r_t the corresponding radii.

In practice, it is convenient to plasmolyse a population of cells in a tissue and then select particular cells for the determination from among those of regular shape which have plasmolysed in a suitable form. With the onion epidermal cells, which have fairly rigid walls, V_t can be calculated accurately enough by estimating l_t from the position of the cell walls in the plasmolysed cell (Fig. 4–3a) and taking r_t as equal to r_p. If desired, l_t and r_t can be measured after subsequent deplasmolysis.

Because of inherent inaccuracies in the available methods, it is impossible to determine the exact osmotic potential of vacuolar sap *in situ*. The term 'osmotic value' is sometimes applied to the estimates of osmotic potential that are made. The osmotic value determined by different methods may be expected to differ because of the different errors inherent in the various techniques.

4.6 Measurement of water potential

The water potential of the vacuolar sap determines the ability of a cell to take up water. Water is absorbed from a solution of higher water potential and released to one of lower water potential than the sap. Most methods of estimating the water potential of vacuolar sap involve determination of the water potential of a medium in which a cell neither takes up nor loses water. It is difficult, if not impossible, to determine water potential of vacuolar sap in an intact multicellular plant and since the potential may change immediately upon excision, e.g. by release of tissue tensions, evaporation, etc., measurements made on isolated groups of cells are no more than a rough approximation to the true values *in situ*.

The following methods can be used to estimate the uptake or loss of water by tissues.

(a) Volume methods

A method based on measurement of changes in the linear dimensions when cells are placed in solutions of different osmotic potential was used first by URSPRUNG and BLUM to determine the 'suction pressure' of individual cells. The method may be modified to enable the mean water potential of a population of cells to be estimated. Strips of homogeneous tissue about 2 cm long and 2 mm wide are removed from the plant organ and transferred to a glass plate. The length of each strip is measured as accurately as possible using a millimetre scale and the strips are then placed in a series of sucrose solutions for about 1 hour. The strips are then re-measured and the results plotted graphically. The water potential of the solution in which the strips do not change in length is taken to be the same as that of the strips (Fig. 4–5).

If the structure of a tissue is inhomogeneous such that it is prevented from swelling or contracting on one side, e.g. by the presence of a rigid cuticle or thick-walled cells, the water potential of cells on the other side can be judged roughly from the degree of curvature which results when pieces of tissue are immersed in solutions of different osmotic potential A solution in which a straight piece of tissue does not curve has a water potential approximately the same as that of the cells under investigation. Segments of pea stem inter-nodes, dock leaf petioles and dandelion peduncles, cut longitudinally into quadrants can be used to demonstrate this method.

(b) Gravimetric method

Pieces of tissue are weighed quickly on a sensitive balance and placed in graded series of solutions of sucrose or other suitable solute. After equili-bration the experimental material is removed, dried rapidly between filter

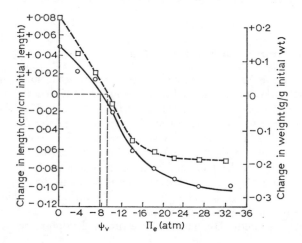

Fig. 4–5 Determination of the water potential of potato tuber tissue by the volume (□– – – – –□) and weighing (O———O) methods. (Data of MEYER and WALLACE, 1941.) For explanation, see text.

papers, and weighed again. The solution in which no change in weight occurs is taken to have a water potential corresponding to that of the tissue (Fig. 4–5).

Success of the gravimetric method depends on the rapidity with which the weighings are made and standardization of the drying procedure. Good results can be obtained by using a sensitive spring balance with which it is possible to weigh a leaf, or a single slice of a storage organ quickly. The method tends to give an over-estimate for storage tissue slices because displacement of air from intercellular spaces causes some increase in weight when a slice is placed in a solution having the same water potential as the vacuolar sap.

(c) Refractometric method

This method involves immersing pieces of tissue in solutions of varying osmotic potential and determining the solution in which there is no change in concentration as measured by a refractometer. STOCKING (1945) devised a procedure for determining the water potential of pith cells in intact *Cucurbita* plants by this method. Sugar solutions of known concentration are injected into the hollow petioles and at intervals samples are withdrawn for examination. When no change in refractive index is observed, it is concluded that the potential of the solution is the same as that of cells at the inner surface of the petiole.

(d) *Vapour pressure methods*

The principle of these methods is that water will not be lost or gained by a tissue from moist air when the vapour pressure of the air corresponds to the potential of water in the tissue. (cf. p. 14.) One method is to place the material (e.g. leaf discs) on small grids above the surface of salt solutions of known osmotic potential and measure the change in weight after a period of equilibration at constant temperature. Another method, devised by SPANNER (1951), makes use of the cooling caused by evaporation of water from the junction of a sensitive thermocouple. The thermocouple is placed in an enclosed space with a piece of plant tissue from which water evaporates at a rate depending on the water potential of the tissue. Temperature changes in the thermocouple are recorded on a galvanometer and the system is calibrated using solutions of known osmotic potential in place of tissue.

The main advantages of the vapour pressure methods are that immersion of the tissue in an aqueous solution is avoided and the determination can be repeated several times on the same piece of tissue. With a well designed psychrometer equilibrium is established in about 15 minutes.

(e) *Chardakov's method*

This method requires only the simplest apparatus and is extremely reliable. A range of mannitol solutions is prepared and 10 ml of each solution is taken to act as a control. To each control a drop of concentrated dye, e.g. methylene blue, is added. Cut pieces of tissue are immersed in unstained aliquots of the mannitol solutions and allowed to equilibrate. The tissue is then removed and a drop of coloured solution is added carefully from a pipette below the surface of the solution to each test tube. If water has been absorbed by the material the test solution will have become more concentrated and hence more dense, and the blue colour will tend to rise, whereas if water has been lost from the tissue, causing dilution of the solution, the coloured drop will sink to the bottom. The osmotic potential of the solution in which the coloured solution diffuses out of the drop without tendency to rise or fall is taken to be equal to the water potential of the tissue.

4.7 Non-osmotic water absorption

It was observed by BENNET-CLARK, GREENWOOD and BARKER (1936) that the apparent mean osmotic potential of cell sap determined by the method of limiting plasmolysis was often lower than that determined cryoscopically on sap extracted from the same tissue (Table 9). Furthermore, they showed that red beet root cells cannot usually be plasmolysed in samples of sap extracted from the same tissue. From these observations they concluded that another factor in addition to the osmotic potential of the vacuolar sap and turgor pressure contributes to the absorption of water by cells. They suggested that this factor might be a 'secretion force' due to the existence of a mechanism pumping water actively into the vacuole, with expenditure of metabolic energy (cf. active transport of solutes, p. 17).

Table 9 A comparison of the osmotic potentials (OP) of vacuolar sap determined by cryoscopy of expressed sap, and by the method of limiting plasmolysis. (Data from BENNET-CLARK, GREENWOOD and BARKER, 1936.)

Tissue		OP of expressed sap (atm)	External OP at limiting plasmolysis (atm)	Apparent additional potential causing water uptake (atm) *
Beta vulgaris	A	− 15·5	− 23·4	− 7·1
(red beet root)	B	− 9·5	− 12·6	− 2·6
	C	− 12·0	− 18·4	− 5·8
Brassica	A	− 11·4	− 17·8	− 5·9
hapobrassica	B	− 11·85	− 17·0	− 4·6
(swede roots)				
Begonia rex	A	− 5·3	− 8·0	− 2·4
	B	− 5·5	− 8·0	− 2·2
	A	− 7·5	− 8·1	− 0·2
	B	− 8·6	− 9·5	− 0·5
Caladium sp.	A	− 5·8	− 5·5	− 0·5
	B	− 5·8	− 6·4	− 0·4

* These values are corrected to allow for the difference in cell volume between full turgidity and limited plasmolysis.

Since cytoplasm is much more permeable to water than to dissolved substances (see Chapter 3, p. 13) a great deal more energy would need to be expended to maintain a concentration gradient for water than say for inorganic salts. LEVITT (1947) calculated that the whole of the energy released from respiration in a red beet root cell is insufficient to maintain a gradient of water potential of more than about 1 atmosphere. This led him to think that deficiencies in the methods employed must be responsible for the discrepancies observed by BENNET-CLARK and his collaborators. Sources of error might include dilution of vacuolar sap during expression, penetration of plasmolyticum, and neglect of matric potential caused by presence of hydrophilic colloids, e.g. proteins in the sap.

There is a considerable amount of evidence that water uptake by cells is somehow related to respiration and this has sometimes been taken to indicate that non-osmotic water absorption occurs. Aerobic conditions promote water uptake by roots and absorption is reduced at low temperature and by respiratory poisons. However, low temperature, lack of oxygen and respiratory inhibitors apparently increase the resistance of cytoplasm to water flow so that the observation that water uptake is affected by such treatments does not prove that active processes are directly involved. Moreover, inhibition of respiration reduces the active transport of solutes into the vacuole, and this in turn may affect the osmotic potential of vacuolar sap and hence the absorption of water.

Growth-promoting substances, such as indole acetic acid (IAA) and naphthalene acetic acid (NAA) stimulate absorption of water by plant cells which are capable of growth. This fact has sometimes been taken to indicate that water absorption occurs actively. However, it now seems clear that the principal effect of the auxins in stimulating water uptake is to cause an increase in the extensibility of the cell wall with consequent reduction in turgor pressure (THIMANN and SAMUEL, 1955) and decrease in water potential. The continued absorption of water by growing cells occurs along a gradient of water potential maintained partly by continued accumulation of solutes in the vacuole and partly by growth of the wall.

For the reasons given above, it seems unlikely that active water movement is a significant factor in the water relations of parenchyma cells, but this does not remove the possibility that it is important in specialized cells, e.g. in water-excreting glands such as hydathodes which occur in the leaves of

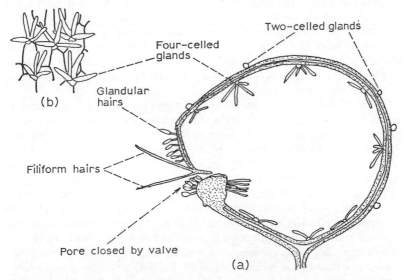

Fig. 4–6 (a) Longitudinal section through a bladder of *Utricularia* sp. (b) Surface of view of the inner wall of a bladder. (Redrawn from ARBER, 1925)

some plants. Water excretion appears to be involved in the mechanism for trapping small aquatic animals in the bladder-wort (*Utricularia* spp.) where gland cells line the inner and outer walls of the bladder (Fig. 4–6). The bladder communicates with the exterior through a pore which can be closed by a water-tight valve-like structure. With the pore closed, the trap is set by excretion of water through the walls of the bladder which occurs to such an extent that the volume of water in the vesicle may be reduced to as little as one half. This causes the wall of the bladder to cave inwards and a negative pressure is developed. When a small animal touches a hair on the door of the trap, the door opens releasing the tension and the victim is sucked into the bladder in a stream of water. An electrical potential difference has been observed between the internal and external solution (outside −ve by some 40–110 mV) and it has been suggested that water is transported into the bladder by electrosmosis. (See p. 21.) This requires further investigation.

Electro-osmosis has also been invoked to explain the observation that seed coats are more permeable to water in one direction than the other. BRAUNER (1930) observed that if seed coats of horsechestnut (*Aesculus hippocastanum*) are treated with potassium sulphate which apparently reverses the electrical charges on the pores of the membrane, the polarity of water permeability is also reversed.

SCHOLANDER (1955) observed that the liquid endosperm ('milk') in coconuts is held under hydrostatic pressure which varies inversely with the nut size, being about 5 atm in small coconuts to 2 atm in large ones. The osmotic potential of the milk was found to be about −7 atm in both small and large nuts and so if the nuts were behaving as simple osmometers they would be expected to develop the same hydrostatic pressure. SCHOLANDER concluded that there may be a water secretory process located in the nut which is partly responsible for the development of hydrostatic pressure in coconuts. Alternatively the results might be attributable to higher matrice potentials in young nuts.

Of great interest are the rather rapid changes in turgidity which occur in specialized 'motor cells' such as the 'hinge cells' which occur in the upper surface of grass leaves causing them to fold up under dry conditions, and the pulvinus cells in the sensitive plant, *Mimosa pudica*, which are responsible for depression of the leaf petiole and the folding of the leaflets in response to touch. Various workers have concluded that rapid loss of turgidity which occurs in these cells is caused by active excretion of water. WEINTRAUB (1952) claimed that contractile vacuoles may be involved in this process and a similar suggestion has been made to account for the loss of water in the process that occurs during the development of a zygote, e.g. in *Spirogyra*. Although the importance of contractile vacuoles in regulating the water content of some protozoa (e.g. *Amoeba*) and algae (e.g. *Chlamydomonas* spp.) is well known the existence of such organelles in higher plant cells has not yet been demonstrated convincingly.

The Mechanism of Stomatal Movement

5.1 Morphology of stomata

The surface of the aerial parts of vascular plants is perforated by small pores, the *stomata*, through which gaseous exchange occurs. They vary considerably in distribution, size and frequency as Table 10 shows, and also in structure (Fig. 5–1). Each stoma is bounded by two 'guard' cells and

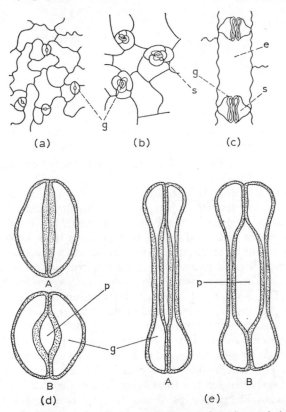

(a)   (b)   (c)

(d)   (e)

Fig. 5–1 Morphology of stomata. (a) *Tropaeolum* (no subsidiary cells); (b) *Sedum* (three subsidiary cells of unequal size surrounding each stoma); (c) *Zea* (dumb-bell shaped guard cells and paired subsidiary cells typical of grasses); (d) *Allium* stoma in the closed (A) and open (B) position; (e) 'Grass-type' stoma in the closed (A) and open (B) position.
g = guard cell; s = subsidiary cell; e = epidermal cell; p = pore.

Table 10　Size and distribution of stomata on leaves of various plants

Size is expressed as length × breadth of the pore when fully open; spacing is the mean distance between the centres of neighbouring stomata

Species	Mean stomatal number per cm^2		Mean size (μ)	Spacing on lower epidermis (μ)
	Upper epidermis	Lower epidermis		
Bean (Phaseolus vulgaris)	4000	28100	7 × 3	67·5
Ivy (Hedera helix)	0	15800	11 × 4	90·0
Maize (Zea mays)	5200	6800	19 × 5	137
Tomato (Lycopersicon esculentum)	1200	13000	13 × 6	99·2
Wheat (Triticum sativum)	3300	1400	18 × 7	302
Sunflower (Helianthus annus)	8500	15600	22 × 8	90·5
Oat (Avena sativa)	2500	2300	38 × 8	235·8
Geranium (Pelargonium sp.)	1900	5900	24 × 9	146·0
Wandering Jew (Zebrina pendula)	0	1400	31 × 12	302

additional epidermal cells termed 'subsidiary cells' may be associated with them (Fig. 5–1 (b), (c)).

The size of the aperture is controlled by alteration in the size and shape of the guard cells, resulting from changes in their water content. In dicotyledons, the walls of the guard cells are usually unevenly thickened, the dorsal wall, i.e. the one away from the pore, being thinner than the ventral wall. With increase in turgor of the guard cells relative to that of surrounding cells, the dorsal walls become more convex, drawing the ventral walls apart to open the pore. Conversely, when the guard cells become less turgid, the pore closes (Fig. 5–1(d)). It has been estimated from microscopical observations that guard cells may increase in volume by as much as 25 per cent when the stomata open (SCARTH and SHAW, 1951). More complicated stomata occur in grasses and sedges (Fig. 5–1 (c), (e)). Here a pair of subsidiary cells are more prominent than the guard cells, which are approximately dumbbell shaped. The dilated ends of the guard cells have thin walls while the narrow intervening region has thick walls. When the guard cells take up water the thin-walled parts expand and the thickened regions move apart (Fig. 5–1(e)).

5.2　Patterns of stomatal response

Changes in the turgidity of guard cells, with consequent alteration in size of the stomatal pore, occur in response to a variety of external stimuli, the most important of which are light, carbon dioxide concentration and water supply (Fig. 5–2). Several diurnal patterns of stomatal behaviour are observed. In most thin-leaved mesophytes, when water supply is adequate, the stomata tend to open during day-time in response to light, and close at night. If moisture conditions become less favourable, so that the leaves lose turgor, the stomata may close partially or completely for a time in the middle of the day. This is perhaps because photosynthesis is reduced and the concentration of carbon dioxide in the intercellular spaces rises. Such mid-day closure is often accompanied by a transitory opening during the night. In most cereals, e.g. barley, wheat, oats, the stomata hardly ever open at night and many of them remain closed during most of the day. In contrast, there are some plants, including potato and onion, in which the stomata are continually open under favourable moisture conditions, except for a few hours

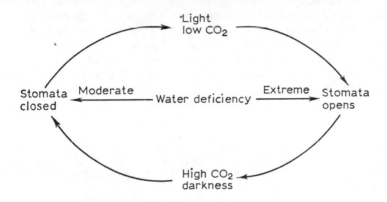

Fig. 5–2   Normal response of stomata to light, carbon dioxide concentration and water deficiency.

immediately after sun-set. Mid-day closure does not occur in these plants until they are visibly wilted, and under extreme conditions of water deficit opening may occur during the normal closure period. In succulent plants (e.g. cacti and *Sedum* spp.) and other xerophytes, a quite different pattern of stomatal behaviour is observed; the stomata commonly open at night and close by day.

The basis of these different patterns of stomatal response is not yet understood, but it seems to be related to the sensitivity of guard cells to changing carbon dioxide level in the intercellular spaces of the leaf (see below).

5.3 Measurement of stomatal size

(i) Direct measurement under the microscope

It is often possible to measure the size of individual pores under the microscope, using an eyepiece micrometer. The method cannot be used very conveniently on plants with hairy leaves or when the stomata are sunk in pits. Manipulation of the leaf in preparation for microscopic examination may disturb the condition of the stomata before they can be measured. One method of minimizing this error is to cut the leaf quickly into small pieces which are then immersed in liquid paraffin and examined at leisure. There is great variation between individual stomata on a single leaf and it is a tedious business measuring enough pores to get a mean value of stomatal size for the leaf as a whole. It is sometimes possible to photograph the leaf surface under the microscope and make measurements on a suitably enlarged print.

(ii) Lloyd's method

LLOYD (1908) claimed that if strips of epidermis are removed from fresh leaves and immersed in absolute alcohol very quickly, the stomata are fixed in the condition occurring at the moment of stripping. An advantage of this method is that measurements under the microscope can be postponed, but the labour involved in obtaining mean values is not reduced. LLOYD'S method only gives reliable results for plants with an easily detachable epidermis. HEATH (1959) is of the opinion that the method is useful as an indication of trends in the opening and closure of stomata in *Pelargonium*, but cannot be used to obtain quantitative data.

(iii) Use of surface replicas

An impression of the leaf surface can be made on dental wax. The impression is then covered with a thin film of cellulose acetate (clear nail varnish works very well) which is allowed to harden and peeled off for microscopic examination.

(iv) Infiltration methods

If a drop of liquid of sufficiently low surface tension is applied to the surface of a leaf with open stomata, it penetrates into the intercellular spaces and the infiltrated area appears translucent. Pores which are fully open allow liquids to enter which have such a high surface tension that they are incapable of penetrating partly-closed stomata. By examining the degree of penetration of a graded series of liquids it is possible to estimate the size of the stomata. MOLISCH (1912) used mixtures of absolute alcohol, benzol and xylol for this purpose, and recently even more suitable liquids have been recommended (ALVIM and HAVIS, 1954).

As an alternative procedure, a single liquid can be applied and the percentage of leaf area injected in a given time measured. When the stomata are fully open, penetration occurs more rapidly than when they are partly closed. If a dye is added to the penetrating liquid the area injected can be estimated more easily. WILLIAMS (1949) recommended a strong solution of gentian violet in absolute alcohol which makes the injected patches show clearly even in dried pressed leaves.

An advantage of the infiltration method is that it yields information about the mean size of thousands of stomata from a single observation. The measurements must first be calibrated against stomatal size by observations on leaves with pores of known size, as estimated by methods (i), (ii) or (iii) above.

(v) Porometers

The *porometer*, first devised by DARWIN and PERTZ (1911), is an apparatus for measuring the rate at which air is drawn through a leaf under the influence of a small pressure difference. The rate of air-flow depends partly on the resistance offered by the stomata and hence on pore size. In the simplest porometer, a small chamber is attached by an air-tight joint to a leaf surface.

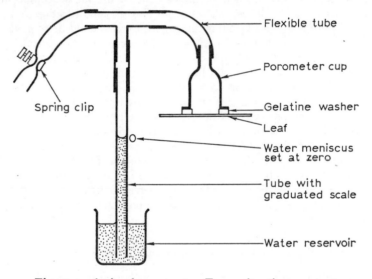

Fig. 5–3   A simple porometer. For explanation, see text.

Air is drawn into the leaf through stomata outside the cup, passes through intercellular spaces and then out of the leaf into the chamber along a pressure gradient caused by a column of water of given height (Fig. 5–3). The rate at which the water column falls can be used to estimate the mean size of stomata in the neighbourhood of the porometer cup. The readings must be calibrated by direct microscopic observations of pore size on the same leaf.

Various modifications have been devised to improve the accuracy and convenience of the porometer method. These include a constant *pressure porometer* (KNIGHT, 1915) which employs suction to maintain a pressure gradient and overcomes the disadvantage of having a decreasing pressure difference as the water column falls. In the *resistance porometer* (GREGORY and PEARSE, 1934; SPANNER and HEATH, 1951) the calculations of stomatal size are based on pressure differences measured by two manometers. The *Wheatstone bridge porometer* (HEATH and RUSSELL, 1951) represents another improvement in convenience and sensitivity. BIERHUIZEN, SLATYER and ROSE (1965) have described a sensitive porometer which can be connected to a blood pressure meter for use in the field.

A disadvantage of porometer methods in general is that the resistance measured is that of the intercellular spaces through which the air travels, as well as of the stomata; and the value of the former is not always constant. This error is reduced when stomata are present on both sides of the leaf because the intercellular path is then shorter.

The presence of the porometer chamber may alter the condition of the stomata within it by reducing light intensity and by altering the composition of the enclosed air with respect to carbon dioxide concentration and humidity. In order to minimize this difficulty the cup should be removed in the intervals between porometer readings when experiments are prolonged.

Physiologists are generally interested, not so much in absolute stomatal sizes or their resistance to mass flow, but in the resistance presented to diffusion, i.e. '*diffusion resistance*' or '*conductance*'. The porometers described above give measurements of resistance to mass flow from which pore sizes and diffusion rates can be calculated, but attempts have also been made to devise '*diffusion porometers*' where diffusive resistance is estimated more directly. In general, these involve measurements of the rate at which a gas, for example hydrogen, diffuses from one side of a leaf to the other. So far, diffusion porometers have proved of greatest use in relating the readings of the much more convenient mass-flow porometers to diffusion resistance.

For further details of the design and use of porometers reference may be made to HEATH (1959) and to MEIDNER (1965).

5.4   Mechanism of stomatal opening and closure

Guard cells differ from other epidermal cells in that they contain chloroplasts and an early hypothesis of stomatal opening due to VON MOHL was that photosynthesis causes an increase in turgor in the guard cells by the synthesis of osmotically-active substances. It was not until nearly 100 years later that it was confirmed by use of radioactively-labelled carbon dioxide that guard cells are capable of photosynthesis, but that it occurs at a rate which is much too slow to account for the maximum rates of osmotic potential change necessary to cause opening (SHAW and MACLACHLAN, 1954).

Long before this, others had suspected that photosynthesis in guard cells was insufficient to account for stomatal movement and LLOYD (1908) put forward the hypothesis that the turgidity of guard cells is controlled by a change of osmotic potential caused by the interconversion of starch and sugar. It has often been observed that starch tends to disappear when stomata open and to increase when they close. The diurnal changes in starch/

sugar balance occurring in guard cells are the converse of those which take place in other cells of the leaf.

SAYRE (1926) investigated the effects of pH on stomatal movement and starch content of the guard cells in strips of epidermis from *Rumex patientia*. He found that the widest stomatal opening occurred at pH 4·2–4·4 where starch content was minimal. At higher and lower pH values than these, stomatal closure occurred and this was associated with an increase in starch content. From such observations, SAYRE concluded that stomatal opening was caused by an increase in pH which favours the hydrolysis of guard-cell starch to sugar and thus lowers the osmotic potential. He suggested that light might instigate these effects by removing carbonic acid through photosynthesis. Following the demonstration in plant tissues of the enzyme starch phosphorylase (HANES, 1940), which catalyses the reaction

$$\text{Starch} + n(\text{inorganic phosphate}) \rightleftharpoons n(\text{glucose-1-phosphate})$$

it was concluded that this enzyme is involved in the starch–sugar interconversion in guard cells. Later, evidence was obtained that the enzyme actually occurs in guard cells (YIN and TUNG, 1948). It should be noted that the phosphorylase reaction alone cannot cause the required change in osmotic potential because for every molecule of glucose-1-phosphate produced an ion of inorganic phosphate disappears so that the number of particles in the solution is hardly changed. If by further reactions the glucose-1-phosphate is hydrolysed to glucose and inorganic phosphate a decrease in osmotic potential will occur. Although the starch $\rightleftharpoons$ sugar hypothesis has much to recommend it, it must be emphasized that starch content and degree of stomatal opening cannot always be correlated, e.g. during mid-day closure. There are some guard cells, e.g. in the onion, in which starch has never been found; in such cases other polysaccharides, e.g. fructose, are present which could act in the same way.

Effect of carbon dioxide concentration

When plants are put in carbon dioxide-free air the stomata tend to stay open even in the dark. Conversely, an increase in carbon dioxide concentration above that normally present in air causes stomata to close even in the light. Because of the sensitivity of stomata to carbon dioxide concentration it may happen that the condition of stomata enclosed in a porometer cup is quite different from that of stomata freely exposed to the air. This is something which needs to be checked when determining stomatal apertures by the porometer method (see p. 42).

There is evidence that the carbon dioxide concentration in the intercellular spaces of the leaf in the vicinity of a stoma is of greater significance than the carbon dioxide concentration elsewhere in the leaf or in the air outside. If the stomata of a plant have been closed by exposing them to high carbon dioxide levels, they do not re-open readily when transferred to carbon dioxide-free air in the dark presumably because the carbon dioxide level

4—P.W.

in the intercellular spaces remains high. If the plant is illuminated, re-opening occurs because the level of carbon dioxide within the leaf is reduced through photosynthesis. It has been observed that the opening stimulus can be transmitted from illuminated to darkened leaves of a plant and it is thought that this occurs by establishment of gradients of carbon dioxide concentration between the illuminated and darkened regions which results in a gradual reduction of the carbon dioxide level in the darkened leaves. In variegated leaves, it is found that stomata in the non-chlorophyllous regions respond on exposure to light or darkness in the same way as those in the green regions, but do so more slowly. This can be attributed to a delay in the lowering of the carbon dioxide level in the intercellular spaces in the non-photosynthetic region of the leaf.

Effects of water stress

If a plant is losing more water through transpiration than is being ab-sorbed, a water deficit gradually develops and this tends to cause stomatal closure irrespective of light and carbon dioxide concentration. It has been shown that this movement is often accompanied by conversion of sugar to starch in the guard cells (YEMM and WILLIS, 1954). It is a striking and un-explained fact that these changes in stomatal starch induced by wilting are the reverse of those occurring at the same time in mesophyll cells of the leaf (cf. p. 43). There, starch is hydrolysed on wilting thus decreasing the water potential of the leaf cells. Attempts to determine whether the stomatal responses to water deficit are due to induced changes in carbon dioxide concentration resulting from reduced photosynthesis have so far yielded inconclusive results.

When a leaf wilts rapidly, there may be an opening response before the stomata close. This has been attributed to a more rapid loss of turgor by the surrounding epidermal cells than by the guard cells, causing the guard cells to swell temporarily. Conversely, when a water deficit is made up rapidly, turgor often increases more quickly in the surrounding cells than in the guard cells so that a temporary closing reaction may occur before the opening response. A greater loss of turgidity in the adjacent epidermal cells than in the guard cells is thought to be responsible for the permanent opening of stomata which sometimes occurs when wilting is prolonged (Fig. 5–2).

Response to temperature

Within the range of about 10–25°C, the effect of temperature is mainly to influence the rate of the opening and closing reactions. At low temperatures stomata behave more sluggishly than at higher temperatures where move-ment occurs quickly. Temperatures above about 25°C tend to cause closure under any conditions, and in the onion HEATH (1952) attributed this to increased carbon dioxide concentration due to a greater stimulation of respiration than of photosynthesis. He found that if the interior of an onion leaf was swept with carbon dioxide-free air, closure did not occur until the temperature was increased to above 35°C. He also suggested that mid-day closure of onion stomata might be the result of high temperature causing increased internal carbon dioxide concentration.

Autonomous diurnal rhythms

The stomata of a number of plant species have been observed to show a 24-hour cycle of movement, even under constant environmental conditions. This rhythm has presumably been imposed on the plant by the regular alternation of light and darkness to which it was previously exposed. This autonomous rhythm of opening and closure appears to be correlated with rhythmic changes in the starch $\rightleftharpoons$ sugar balance, and tends to disappear gradually when the plant is kept for a prolonged period under constant environmental conditions.

Active water movement

In the section above, it was postulated that movement of water into and out of the guard cells is a response to changes in water potential induced by alteration in the starch–sugar balance. However, the possibility that active water movements are involved cannot be excluded. WILLIAMS (1954) suggested that the loss of turgidity in guard cells, which results in stomatal closure, is an active process involving excretion of water from the cells by a mechanism which requires metabolic energy (see p. 34). Opening, on the other hand, is the result of a return of the guard cells to normal turgidity when excretion stops. If WILLIAMS' hypothesis is correct, the closure of stomata should be prevented by lack of oxygen. HEATH and ORCHARD (1956) tested this possibility on wheat and found, on the contrary, that lack of oxygen induced closure. These results indicate that there might be active uptake of water *during* opening, but in the absence of direct evidence it seems more probable that anaerobic conditions cause closure either by interfering with the starch $\rightleftharpoons$ sugar balance or by causing an increase in osmotic potential of the guard cells in some other way.

Active salt movement

It has been known for many years that alkali cations, particularly sodium and potassium ions stimulate the opening of stomata in detached epidermal strips. It is possible that changes in the water potential of guard cells during stomatal movement are due, at least partly to transport of these ions into and out of the vacuoles.

Transpiration 6

6.1 Measurement of transpiration

That a plant gives off water vapour can be demonstrated quite simply by watering it well and putting it in an enclosed space, for example under a bell jar, when after a time, drops of water will condense on the sides of the vessel. STEPHEN HALES, who was among the first men to study the physiology of plants scientifically, described such an experiment in his book 'Vegetable Staticks' (1727), which everyone interested in plant physiology should read. HALES devised a variety of means of measuring the amount of water lost by a transpiring plant, and these are basically the methods still in use today. Although the techniques employed have been refined in the intervening years, a basic difficulty still remains in all measurements of transpiration, namely, that placing a plant under conditions necessary for measurement affects the transpiration rate. The various methods available are as follows:

(a) Loss in weight of a potted plant

The transpiration rate of a potted plant can be estimated by measuring the loss in weight of a plant and its container, over convenient intervals of time. It is necessary to prevent evaporation from the soil by covering it with waterproofed material, and if a clay pot is used this must also be enclosed. It is advisable to employ a fairly large quantity of soil to prevent it drying out too much during prolonged experiments and this means that a balance capable of recording heavy weights with reasonable accuracy is required. The transpiration rates of young trees growing in vessels containing up to 1000 lb of soil have been measured successfully but clearly the method is more suitable for small plants. It can be adapted for use with plants growing in solution culture.

An inherent error in this method is that the loss of water through transpiration during an experiment is partly compensated for by an increase in weight of the plant resulting from growth and so the estimates of water loss are inevitably too small. However, this error is usually less than those associated with weighing and often it can be neglected.

(b) Loss in weight of excised shoots or leaves

A leaf or branch is cut off and weighed on a sensitive spring balance at intervals of 1 or 2 minutes (HUBER, 1927; STOCKER, 1956). The results are plotted graphically, and the line joining the points is extrapolated to zero time. The initial slope of the line is taken to represent the transpiration rates immediately before excision (Fig. 6-1). The method gives a satisfactory estimate of water loss from the organ *in situ* when the plant is not suffering from a water deficit, but if an appreciable water deficit exists within the

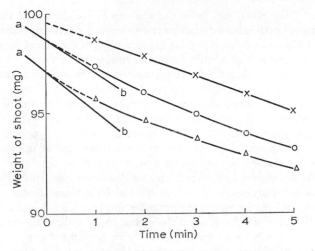

Fig. 6–1 Determination of the transpiration rate of a cut shoot by rapid weighing at short intervals. X——X, ⊙——⊙, △——△, are measurements made on different shoots. When the graph is curved the initial slope is calculated by drawing a tangent (a–b) to the curve at zero time.

plant there is such a marked increase in transpiration rate due to release of tensions in the water columns immediately upon excision that a serious error is introduced. The method has been widely used, particularly in ecological work, and has provided useful comparative data (Table 11).

Table 11 Relative rates (Spruce = 100) of transpiration of various trees as measured by different methods. (From HUBER, 1953)

	Weighed potted seedlings (Eidmann)	Rapid weighing of detached twigs	
		(Pisek and Cartellière)	(Polster)
Spruce (*Picea abies*)	100	100	100
Scots pine (*Pinus sylvestris*)	181	133	139
Larch (*Larix europaea*)	310	212	212
Beech (*Fagus sylvatica*)	268	377	372
Oak (*Quercus robur*)	286	512	460
Birch (*Betula verrucosa*)	618	541	740

(c) Freeman's method (FREEMAN, 1908)

The plant, or part of it, is enclosed in a glass vessel through which a stream of dry air is allowed to flow. The water vapour is collected in tubes containing phosphorus pentoxide or calcium chloride and weighed. In a control experiment the same volume of air is drawn through a similar apparatus in the absence of the plant, and from the changes in weight of the two sets of collecting tubes the amount of water transpired in a given time is determined. The technique can be modified for measurement of the rate of water loss by a single leaf, or part of a leaf, of a plant growing in the field.

More recently various kinds of hygrometers have been designed to estimate the water content of air after it has passed over the plant. These include the use of wet and dry thermocouples (GLOVER, 1941), measurement of infra-red absorption (SCARTH, LOEWY and SHAW, 1948; DECKER and WIEN, 1960) and the corona hygrometer (ANDERSSON, HERTZ and RUFELT, 1954). FALK (1966) has described a sensitive hygrometer which makes use of microwaves for determining changes in the dielectric properties of the air.

The basic method has several serious disadvantages. In particular the experimental material is placed in a closed container under abnormal conditions of light intensity, temperature and humidity. Light intensity is lowered because of reflection and absorption in the walls of the vessel, while temperature tends to increase, especially in sunlight due to the 'greenhouse' effect. Transpiration is also affected by the rate of air-flow. When the rate of air-flow is rapid and the amount of plant material small, humidity remains low and transpiration is maximal, but with a slow air stream humidity rises and transpiration is reduced.

(d) Colour indicator method

Pieces of filter-paper soaked in a concentrated (3–5 per cent) solution of cobalt chloride, or cobalt thiocyanate, and dried in an oven, are stored in a desiccator. When such paper absorbs moisture the blue colour fades and finally becomes pink. A dry piece of the blue paper is placed on the leaf surface and held in place by two thin pieces of glass clipped above and below. Moisture can be excluded on the side containing the paper by sealing the edges of the glass with petroleum jelly. The time taken for the colour of the paper to change from one standard shade of blue to another is a measure of the amount of water lost by the portion of leaf covered by the paper. The method is basically the same as that used to measure dampness in the walls of buildings, and humidity kits sold for this purpose can be used for determination of transpiration from leaves.

The indicator method often gives a poor estimation of the transpiration rate of the plant as a whole, because beneath the paper, the leaf surface is transpiring into almost completely dry air, whereas elsewhere usually it is not. The technique thus measures the maximum transpiration rate attainable under the most favourable conditions. In such circumstances, transpiration rate depends mainly on the number and condition of the stomata (see p. 59) and the method thus gives an indication of the maximum rates of stomatal transpiration. It can be employed to estimate the extent to which the stomata are open, if the experiment can be completed before the paper causes the stomata to move as a result of being shaded (MILTHORPE, 1955).

(e) *Potometers*

With a potometer the rate of water loss from a plant or cut shoot is determined indirectly by measuring the rate of absorption, making the assumption that absorption balances the water lost in transpiration. The apparatus consists essentially of a water reservoir into which the plant, or its part, is sealed, and to which a glass capillary tube of known bore is attached. A bubble of air is introduced into the tube and its rate of movement across a scale is used as an indication of the rate of transpiration. If the bore of the tube is known the amount of water absorbed in a given time can be calculated.

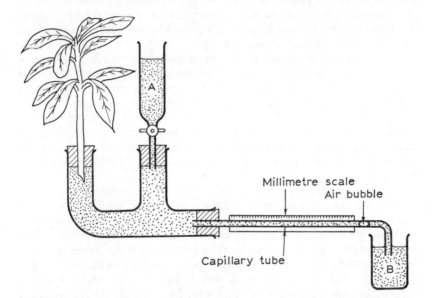

Fig. 6–2 Ganong potometer. A small air-bubble is introduced into the capillary tube by lifting it temporarily out of the water in B. When necessary the bubble can be moved back to the right-hand end of the tube by admitting water from the funnel.

Several different kinds of potometers have been designed for use with both cut shoots and whole plants (Fig. 6–2). Except when experiments are performed at a constant temperature it is desirable to have a control potometer set up nearby, without a plant, to record changes in the volume of water due to thermal variation during an experiment. This is particularly important when the water reservoir is large.

The rate of water uptake by a cut shoot in a potometer is not necessarily that of the same shoot when attached to the plant, because water tensions, in the xylem (see p. 72) and the resistance of the root system to water movement are eliminated by cutting. Gas may be introduced into some of the xylem vessels during excision, rendering them non-functional and thus increasing the overall resistance of the stem. For these reasons it is desirable where possible to use intact plants. Such experiments cannot be prolonged because of the difficulty of providing adequate aeration for the roots.

There is rarely an exact correspondence between transpiration and absorption and especially with whole plants there is often an appreciable lag between a change in transpiration rate and a corresponding change in the rate of absorption. Cut shoots in a potometer generally transpire more quickly than they absorb water and as a result they gradually dry out. If the plant or shoot in a potometer grows during an experiment there is a discrepancy between transpiration and absorption due to retention of water by the growing cells, but the amount of this is usually small, in comparison with the amount of water transpired.

Water loss and absorption can be measured simultaneously by a combination of the weighing and potometer methods. The plant is fixed in a potometer which is weighed at convenient intervals; between weighings, measurements of absorption are made by observing movement of an air bubble in the capillary tube. GREGORY, MILTHORPE, PEARSE and SPENCER (1950) devised an apparatus in which water absorption of a single detached leaf can be measured potometrically, and water loss estimated concurrently by collecting the water vapour evolved in weighed phosphorus pentoxide tubes.

The amount of water transpired in a given time, determined by one or other of the above methods, may be expressed on a per plant basis or alternatively per unit of leaf fresh weight, dry weight or area. Leaf areas can be conveniently measured using a planimeter or by counting the number of unit squares within the leaf outline traced on graph paper. Areas may also be determined by weighing pieces of paper or card cut to the size and the shape of the leaf and computing by comparison with the weight of known areas of the same material. None of these methods is particularly convenient if the leaves are to remain attached to the plant. When it is desired to measure the area of leaves at intervals during an experiment, a photographic method can be used to produce an outline of the leaf on paper. Various types of slow photo-sensitive paper suitable for this purpose are available commercially.

In attempting to understand the factors controlling transpiration it is sometimes convenient to compare the rates of transpiration with evaporation from an atmometer* placed under comparable conditions. The ratio of the two was termed '*transpiration coefficient*' by BRIGGS and SHANTZ (1916) and is sometimes called '*relative transpiration*'. Variation in the value of the coefficient is an indication of the extent to which transpiration is affected by factors other than these which control evaporation, i.e. the degree of control exerted by the plant.

---

* An atmometer, or evaporimeter is an instrument for measuring the rate of evaporation from a porous surface, e.g. porous porcelain kept saturated with water.

6.2 Water consumption by crops and natural vegetation

Agriculturists, foresters and ecologists are often more interested in the total amount of water lost by a stand of vegetation in a given time including that evaporating from the soil than in absolute rates of transpiration. Estimates of such '*evapo-transpiration*' can be made by measuring the differences between precipitation and the run-off of water from a given area over a period of time. On a sloping site where the sub-soil is impervious, run-off can be measured from the rate of flow of streams draining the area. Otherwise, *lysimeters* are constructed in which the drainage water from a given area of soil can be collected periodically and measured. In one type of lysimeter, the soil is enclosed in a concrete tank having an open top and perforated bottom, from which drains run to a collecting vessel. The amount of water supplied to the lysimeter either artificially or as rain is measured and compared with the quantity collected from it over a given time. Generally, it is assumed that the water content of the soil in which plants are growing is the same at the end of the experimental period as at the beginning. Some lysimeters have devices attached to maintain soil moisture at a definite level and others are weighable.

OGATA, RICHARDS and GARDNER (1960) estimated evapo-transpiration by measuring changes in soil moisture content by means of *tensiometers* (see p. 63) under conditions in which loss of water by drainage was negligible. An alternative method under these conditions is to replenish the water supply in the soil regularly in order to keep the soil moisture at a fixed level. Evapo-transpiration can then be equated with the amount of water supplied over the experimental period.

When water is lost by evapo-transpiration, it becomes vaporized and this requires energy. The main source for this energy is direct solar radiation and in England about 40 per cent of the incident energy is available for evaporating water. The rest is reflected or is utilized in photosynthesis and in heating up the soil, air and plants. The amount of available energy sets a maximum value for the rate of evapo-transpiration provided no other factors are limiting. This maximum is called the *potential evapo-transpiration* and has been defined as the amount of water lost in unit time from a given area of ground having a uniform short green crop, e.g. grass, completely covering it, and an adequate supply of soil water. It has been suggested on theoretical grounds that potential evapo-transpiration is largely independent of the type of plant cover and the evidence is that it is relatively constant for a wide range of economic crops. Various meteorological conditions influence potential evaporation (see below) and PENMAN (1948) devised an empirical formula by which it can be calculated from weather data. Estimates of potential evaporation by this formula have given good correlation with the measured consumption of water by agricultural crops in Southern England.

6.3   Environmental factors affecting transpiration

The rate of transpiration characteristically exhibits a diurnal periodicity which is related to various meteorological conditions. In general, transpiration is low at night, increases rapidly after sunrise to a maximum in the late morning or early afternoon and then falls gradually to its low night value (Fig. 6–3). Of the various meteorological factors which fluctuate diurnally, *solar radiation* appears to be most closely correlated with transpiration rates. One reason for this is that sunlight provides energy for evaporation. Since light energy must be absorbed before it can be utilized the colour of an evaporating surface has a marked effect on water loss both from an atmometer and a plant, being greater from a dark absorbing surface

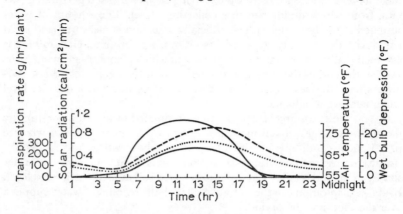

Fig. 6–3   Diurnal fluctuations in transpiration rate of oats (lower continuous line), solar radiation (upper continuous line), air temperature (dashed line) and humidity (dotted line). (Data from BRIGGS and SHANTZ, 1916)

than that from one with high reflectance. Light has a greater effect on transpiration than it has on evaporation from an atmometer and this is attributable to a reduction in the effective evaporating surface of leaves at night by closure of the stomata.

Transpiration occurs more rapidly when the air surrounding a plant is dry, than when it is wet. *Relative humidity* is often used as a measure of water content in air because it can be measured easily. Expressed as a percentage, relative humidity represents the amount of water present in a given volume of air, relative to the amount the air can hold at the same temperature. Transpiration is actually related to the gradient of water potential existing between the air and the evaporating surfaces. It is clear from Table 12 that for a given relative humidity, the vapour pressure difference, and hence water potential gradient is increased with increasing temperature, and so a precise correlation between relative humidity and transpiration can be expected only at a given temperature.

Table 12   Water vapour pressures (mm of mercury) at different temperatures and relative humidities

Temperature (°C)	Vapour pressure 100% relative humidity	60% relative humidity	Vapour pressure difference
10	9·21	5·53	3·68
20	17·54	10·52	7·02
30	31·82	19·09	12·73

If the absolute amount of water in the surrounding air remains constant, an increase in *temperature* raises the vapour pressure of the air slightly, in accordance with Charles' Law, and this has a correspondingly small effect on transpiration. When the temperature of the leaf is higher than that of the air, the water potential gradient is higher than when the temperatures are the same, and in such circumstances a leaf will transpire even into water-saturated air. On the other hand, leaves sometimes become cooler than the air, and in this case dew may be deposited on them under conditions of high humidity.

Air movement over a leaf surface tends to remove water vapour and to increase the water potential gradient, thus promoting transpiration. At high wind speeds, however, transpiration rate may fall because stomatal closure is induced by mechanical disturbance or by incipient drying of the leaf (see p. 44).

If the *availability of water* to a plant is reduced, absorption decreases because of a reduction in the water potential gradient between the soil and root as a result of a decrease in matric potential (see p. 20). An increase in the concentration of soil solution has the same effect. Reduced absorption leads to an increase in the tension of water in the xylem; this causes the potential of water in the leaf cells to decrease and their walls tend to dry out. This increases the resistance of the pathway for diffusion of water from the cells into the intercellular spaces of the leaf, which in turn reduces transpiration. When water stress becomes considerable, the stomata close and this causes a further reduction in transpiration.

6.4 Effects of plant structure on transpiration

Every plant has a characteristic rate of transpiration under a given set of environmental conditions, and this is governed by the structure of its various parts. Of particular importance in this connection are the surface area, external morphology and internal structure of the *leaves*.

In general, plants with a large *area of foliage* transpire more rapidly than those with a smaller leaf area, although per unit of leaf area the rate may be lower. This is because a plant with a large leaf area tends to develop higher water deficits and this tends to reduce transpiration. When a plant is pruned, the rate of transpiration per unit area from the remaining leaves commonly increases somewhat, for the same reason. Plants growing in dry places often shed some of their leaves when water stresses become severe and in this way loss of water is reduced. Reduction of leaf area is one of the characteristic features of xerophytes (see p. 2).

The leaves of different plant species lose water at very different rates when expressed on a unit area basis. Such differences are attributable to *structural features of the leaf* and in particular to the composition of the cuticle; the number, distribution, size and structure of stomata; the area of internal surfaces exposed to the intercellular spaces; and the arrangement

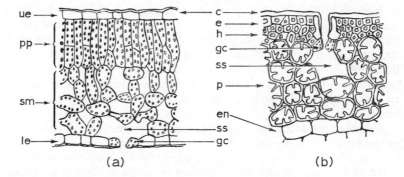

(a)   (b)

Fig. 6–4   Leaf structure. Transverse sections of (a) mesophytic leaf (beech, *Fagus sylvatica*) showing well-differentiated palisade parenchyma and spongy mesophyll; (b) xerophytic leaf (*Pinus nigra*) showing thickened epidermis and hypodermis, sunken stomata and lack of intercellular spaces. c, cuticle; e, epidermis; ue, upper epidermis; le, lower epidermis; h, hypodermis; gc, guard cell; ss, sub-stomatal space; p, parenchyma; pp, palisade parenchyma; sm, spongy mesophyll; en, endodermis.

of vascular tissue. The contrasting appearance of leaves from a plant which loses water quickly and one which transpires slowly are shown in Fig. 6–4. Leaves of the same plant growing under different conditions, e.g. in sun or in shade also show differences in structure, e.g. amount of spongy mesophyll, thickness of cuticle, number of stomata, which affect water loss.

The properties of the *cuticle* profoundly influence transpiration especially at night when the stomata are closed. In shade plants, such as ferns, where the cuticle is thin as much as 30 per cent of the total water lost is transpired through the cuticle (*cuticular transpiration*), while as a contrast, in desert succulents loss through the cuticle is negligible.

The presence of *hairs and scales* on the surface of leaves might be expected to increase transpiration because of the increase in surface area. On the other hand, they tend to reduce transpiration by helping to retain moist air at the leaf surface (see p. 59). Another effect of hairs and scales is to make a leaf surface more reflective, and this may reduce transpiration because of a reduction in absorption of solar radiation (see above). Dense hairiness is often associated with the xerophytic habit which suggests that the first effect is less important than the others.

The leaves of xerophytes sometimes transpire more rapidly per unit of surface area when they are amply supplied with water and the stomata are open, than do mesophytes. TURRELL (1944) attributed this to the greater area of cell walls exposed to the intercellular spaces per unit of leaf area in xerophytes than in mesophytes. The leaves of plants grown at high light intensities also typically have a greater ratio of internal/external surface area than have leaves of the plants of the same species grown in shade, and this may account for the higher rates of transpiration from sun-leaves under some conditions. A greater development of xylem in the leaves of well-illuminated plants may contribute to the effect. Furthermore, leaves grown in sun commonly have a higher density of stomata which may also facilitate transpiration.

Plants which transpire rapidly tend to have more water conducting elements in the *stem* than those which transpire slowly. In the extreme case of submerged aquatic angiosperms vessels may be entirely lacking. The relatively high resistance presented by the tracheid system in gymnosperms compared with the vessels in the xylem of angiosperms (see Chapter 7) may be an important cause of the relatively low transpiration rates characteristic of these plants.

Some water is transpired from the surface of young stems through the cuticle and stomata, but the amount of this is generally small compared with the amounts of water lost from leaves. From older stems, water is lost mainly through the lenticels since the outer layers of the bark consist largely of cork cells in which the walls are impregnated with fats and therefore impermeable to water. *Lenticular transpiration* accounts for most of the water loss from deciduous trees in winter.

Transpiration is reduced if water deficits develop in the plant, and this happens when transpiration is in excess of absorption. Adequate absorption, especially under conditions of low water supply is dependent on a well developed *root system*. Plants growing in dry situations commonly have a better developed root system than these of the same species growing with an abundant water supply, and desert plants in particular are characterized by having very large root-area to shoot-area ratios.

6.5 Diffusion through stomata

Stomata were discovered in the seventeenth century by the Italian microscopist, MALPIGHI, but it was not until the last century that their role in the regulation of transpiration was investigated. Following the observation of von Mohl, and others, that the size of stomata is regulated by light and other factors (see Chapter 5) it was generally accepted that stomatal transpiration is proportional to the number and size of the stomatal pores.

BROWN and ESCOMBE (1900) found that the rate of transpiration from a given area of a sunflower leaf could be as much as one half of the evaporation rate from a free water surface of the same area in spite of the fact that the stomatal pores when fully open occupy less than one per cent of the surface area. In other words, it appeared that water was diffusing through the stomata 50 times more rapidly than from a water surface of area equal to the area of the pores. This discovery led them to investigate the rates of evaporation from water surfaces separated from air of known humidity by thin septa perforated by small pores varying in size, number and in total area. Stefan (1881) had already shown that whereas the rate of diffusion for large bodies of water, such as lakes, is proportional to area, the rate of diffusion from small circular areas is proportional to their perimeter, that is to linear dimensions,

Table 13   Relationship between the loss of water vapour through small openings in membranes and the area and perimeter of the pores. (From SAYRE, 1926)

Diameter of pores (mm)	Loss of water (g)	Relative amounts of water lost	Relative areas of pores	Relative perimeter of pores
2·64	2·66	1·00	1·00	1·00
1·60	1·58	0·59	0·37	0·61
0·95	0·93	0·35	0·13	0·36
0·81	0·76	0·29	0·09	0·31
0·56	0·48	0·18	0·05	0·21
0·35	0·36	0·14	0·01	0·13

rather than to area. BROWN and ESCOMBE confirmed STEFAN's calculations experimentally for the diffusion of water and carbon dioxide, through narrow pores and later workers have obtained similar results (see Table 13).

The interpretation of this effect is that the points of equal water potential over an evaporating area form a series of oblate hemispheres (see Fig. 6–5) and as a result the paths of diffusion of molecules along the water potential gradient are curved. Molecules diffusing from near the edge of the area escape more readily than those nearer the centre because the air is less saturated at a given distance from the evaporating surface near the edge than it is at the centre. The smaller the evaporating area, the greater the proportion of molecules diffusing from near to the edge, and consequently, below a certain size, the rate of evaporation becomes more nearly proportional to linear dimensions than to area.

When a number of small evaporating surfaces are close enough together there is mutual interference between them and the rate of evaporation from each area is reduced (Fig. 6 5 (b)). As the pores approach one another, the loss of water per unit area of evaporating surface approaches that from a single free surface of the same area. VERDUIN (1949) derived a mathematical expression for mutual interference between apertures in multiperforate septa thus:

$$\log Q = \log Q_1 - \frac{k}{D^2}$$

where Q is the diffusion rate per pore; Q_1, the diffusion rate of an isolated pore; D, the distance between pores; and k is a constant. A straight-line

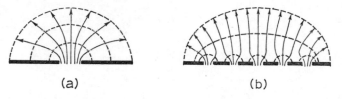

(a)   (b)

Fig. 6–5 Diffusion through small pores in still air. **(a)** Diffusion through a single pore. **(b)** Mutual interference between neighbouring pores. The arrowed lines show directions of diffusion and the dashed lines enclose areas of equal concentration of diffusing molecules. (After BANGE, 1953)

relationship was observed between the log of diffusion rate and the inverse square of the distance between holes thus confirming the equation. Maximum values of Q were obtained for different pore sizes at the following spacings:

                0·8 mm—20 pore diameters
                0·4 mm—30 pore diameters
                0·2 mm—40 pore diameters.

Measurement of stomatal spacing in a variety of plants gave D values ranging from 5·3 to 15·7 diameters. Since the maximum diameter of open stomata is only about 0·04 mm (Table 10, p. 38) it is evident that mutual interference between stomata is high. As stomata close, the spacing increases and interference is reduced. Furthermore, as a stoma closes its pore becomes more elliptical and in consequence the change in perimeter for a given reduction in area is less than it would be if the pore remained spherical. For both these reasons stomatal closure may be expected to exert less control of transpiration than might be expected at least until the pores are nearly closed (see below).

6.6 Control of transpiration

The rate of diffusion of a substance from point A to point B is proportional to the difference in chemical potential between the two points and by the resistance of the intervening pathway (see Chapter 3).

In the case of a leaf the total resistance encountered by a water molecule diffusing from the surface of the leaf cells into the air can be represented by a network of resistances as shown in Fig. 6–6. Assuming that the resistance of the cuticle (R_c) is very high compared with that of the stomata (R_s) and that of intercellular spaces (R_i) is low, the rate of diffusion, i, can be represented thus:

$$i = \frac{\Delta\psi}{R_s + R_a}$$

where $\Delta\psi$ is the difference in water potential across the system and R_a is the resistance of the air above the leaf surface.

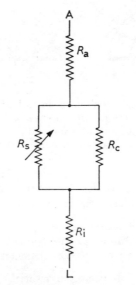

Fig. 6–6   Resistances encountered by a water molecule diffusing from a leaf cell (L) into the surrounding air (A). For explanation, see text.

R_s can be determined by means of porometer measurements (see Chapter 5). Attempts have also been made to calculate R_s from measurements of the physical dimensions of the pores. BROWN and ESCOMBE treated them as tubes with an elliptical cross-section in which case:

$$R_s = \frac{1}{K} \cdot \frac{L}{\pi a b} \cdot \frac{1}{N}$$

where K is the diffusion constant for water vapour; L, the length of the tubes; a, half the short axis of the ellipse; b, half the long axis of the ellipse; and N the number of stomata per unit of surface area. This formula is only an approximation because a stoma is actually irregular in shape having different cross-sections at different distances from the surface.

R_a can also be calculated. BROWN and ESCOMBE separated this resistance into two components—the resistance of the small diffusion zones above each stoma (R_{a_1}) and the resistance of the large diffusion zone above the leaf as a whole (R_{a_2}). For the former they used the formula

$$R_{a_1} = \frac{1}{K} \cdot \frac{1}{4\sqrt{ab}} \cdot \frac{1}{N}$$

This assumes that there is no mutual interference between neighbouring pores. Since interference occurs when stomata are fully open their values for R_{a_1} under these conditions were too high.

R_{a_2} can be calculated from the equation:

$$R_{a_2} = \frac{1}{K} \cdot \frac{1}{4S}$$

where S is the radius of a circular area of leaf under consideration.

The extent to which R_s controls transpiration depends on the relative values of R_s and R_a. In still air, R_a is relatively high and exerts an important effect on transpiration rate. Under these conditions R_s has relatively little influence except when the stomata are nearly closed (Fig. 6–7). On the other

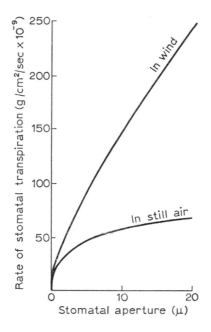

Fig. 6–7 Effect of the size of the stomatal aperture on the rate of stomatal transpiration in *Zebrina* in still air and in wind. (After BANGE, 1953)

5—P.W.

hand when air is moving over the surface of the leaf R_a is much reduced and the size of the stomatal aperture has a much more important effect on water loss. It now becomes clear why there was a considerable divergence of opinion amongst early investigators as to the extent to which stomata exert control over transpiration.

Recognition that R_a may in some circumstances exert a predominant effect on transpiration rate has helped us understand more fully the significance of certain anatomical features characteristic of xerophytes. These plants often have small leaves with a dense covering of leaves or scales, a thick cuticle and sunken stomata, and might be expected to transpire slowly. In fact, it has been shown that in still air when the stomata are open these plants lose as much or more water per unit of surface area as do mesophytes. However, in comparison with mesophytes, wind increases the transpiration of xerophytes relatively little and they also transpire less rapidly than mesophytes when the stomata are closed. In still air, transpiration is largely controlled by R_a which is affected little by the anatomical structure of the leaf. On the other hand, in moving air anything which helps to retain a layer of moist air in the vicinity of the stomata will tend to reduce transpiration. The structure of the cuticle will also be more important in a wind or when the stomata are closed since R_c has a greater influence under these conditions (see Fig. 6-6).

Movement of Water through Plants 7

7.1 Introduction

Being a plant physiologist, I am often asked how water gets to the top of tall trees. The answer to this question is that it flows along a gradient of water potential existing between the soil solution and the air surrounding the plants. As in the case of an electrical current, the rate of flow is dependent on the magnitude of the potential gradient and on the resistance offered by the water pathway. The pathway can be visualized as a system of resistances arranged in series and in parallel (Fig. 7–1). When the potential gradient is large and the resistance low, water flow is rapid and vice-versa.

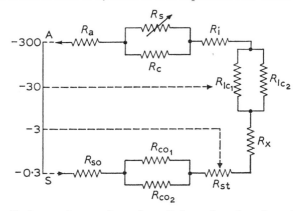

Fig. 7–1 Pathway of water from the soil through a plant into the air showing the main resistances encountered: R_{so}, soil; R_{rco_1}, R_{rco_2}, root cortex; R_{st}, root stele; R_x, conducting elements in the xylem; R_{lc_1}, R_{lc_2}, leaf cortex; R_l, intercellular spaces of the leaves; R_s, stomata; R_c, cuticle; R_a, air above the leaves. The scale shows the approximate drop in water potential across various parts of the system.

R_s is variable through regulation in the size of the stomata. The other resistances in the system are relatively constant although they may alter during the life of a plant, and they are affected to some extent by water tensions developing when water loss exceeds absorption (see p. 72). Much the largest part of the total potential difference in this system occurs across R_l, R_s, R_c and R_a; the difference in water potential between the root and leaf cells of the plant is rarely in excess of about 30 atm, whereas the total potential difference may reach 300 atm, or more. We shall now discuss the pathway of water movement through a plant beginning with a brief consideration of the state of water in soils.

7.2   Availability of soil water

It is common to distinguish four states of water in the soil which differ in their availability to plants.

(i) *Gravitational water* temporarily displaces air from large spaces between the soil particles following rain and gradually percolates downwards under the influence of gravity. If gravitational water remains indefinitely, the soil is said to be water-logged, and it is then unsuitable for growth of most plants because of lack of aeration; some species, e.g. rice (*Orzya sativa*) can grow well under these conditions, probably because the roots are efficiently aerated via the shoots. The submerged parts of some

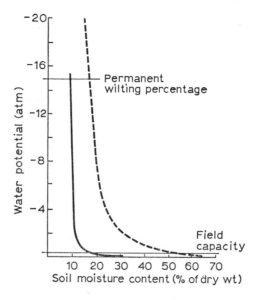

Fig. 7–2   Relationship between water potential and moisture content in a sandy soil (——) and a clay soil (– – – –). (After KRAMER, 1949)

water plants are also supplied with oxygen in this way, and such plants have well-known structural adaptations for the purpose (ARBER, 1925).

(ii) *Capillary water* comprises the bulk of the water remaining in soil after gravitational water has drained away, and is the main source of water for plants. It is held as thin films on the surface of soil particles and in small capillary spaces between them. Soil containing the maximum amount of capillary water and no gravitational water is said to be at its *field capacity*. The field capacity of a clay soil in which the particles are relatively small is greater than that of a sandy soil in which larger particles with a smaller total surface area per unit volume are present (Fig. 7–2) and thus it has a correspondingly greater water storage capacity.

(iii) *Imbibed water*. When soil is allowed to stand in air, water gradually evaporates from it and that which remains in air-dry soil is termed *imbibed* or *hygroscopic* water. It is absorbed by soil colloids and is not easily removed because of the high matric forces by which it is retained (see Chapter 3). This water is mainly unavailable to plants.

(iv) *Water vapour* is present in the air spaces between soil particles in equilibrium with the liquid phase. It is readily absorbed by roots from moist soil, but it is quantitatively a minor source of water to plants.

The *permanent wilting percentage* (PWP) is the water content of a soil (expressed as a percentage of the dry weight) at which the leaves of plants growing in it become wilted and remain so until additional water is added. BRIGGS and SHANTZ (1912) showed that a wide range of plants all reduced the water content of soil to about the same level before permanent wilting occurred. The value of the permanent wilting percentage differs between different soils but the potential of water in a soil at the permanent wilting percentage is usually between about − 10 and − 20 atm (or bars) with a mean value of about − 15 atm. This value is commonly taken in agricultural practice as equivalent to PWP.

Total soil-moisture stress (TSMS) is a term introduced by WADLEIGH and AYERS (1945) to represent the mean potential of water in soil resulting from all the factors which affect it, including gravitational, hydrostatic, matric and osmotic forces. Soil-water potential can be estimated in the laboratory by measuring the relative vapour pressure of the soil water. This involves equilibrating soil samples in small containers at a constant temperature and determining the relative vapour pressure in the air-space above it (RICHARDS and OGATA, 1958). A technique devised by RICHARDS (1965) involving the use of a thermistor hygrometer can be used for determinations of soil-water potential in the field.

Other techniques for the estimation of soil-water potential in the field involve measurement of matric potential using either a tensiometer or conductivity blocks. A tensiometer consists of a water-filled porous ceramic cup which is buried in the soil and connected by water-filled tubing to a manometer or pressure gauge having a calibrated scale from which the potential can be read directly (see RICHARDS, 1949, for details of tensiometer design). The conductivity-block method involves burying in the soil a small block of gypsum or similar porous material containing a pair of electrodes connected to a resistance bridge. The water in the block reaches equilibrium with the soil water and the electrical resistance measured can be related to water potential.

7.3 Movement of water into the stele

Water is absorbed by roots from soil mainly in the region of the *root hairs* (Fig. 7–3(a)). The root hair zone is a particularly favourable one for absorption because it presents a large surface area in intimate contact with water films surrounding the soil particles (Fig. 7–3(b)). Individual root hairs probably function for only a few days, being replaced progressively by others near the tip of the root as it grows. In this way the root-hair zone is brought progressively into contact with new regions of the soil.

Plants grown in solution culture commonly lack root hairs as do the roots of aquatic plants. In these cases, water absorption takes place over the

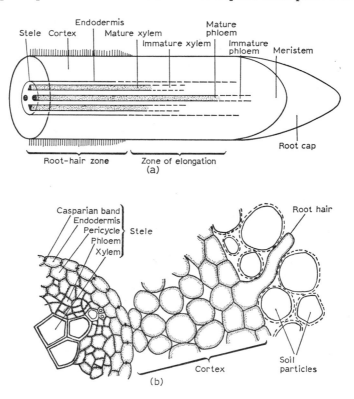

Fig. 7–3 Root structure. (a) Root tip showing various zones, and the regions of differentiation of xylem and phloem. (b) Transverse section of a root in the root hair zone.

whole surface of the root as indeed it does to some extent also in plants growing in soil. There appears to be an appreciable absorption of water through the suberized surfaces of older tree roots, and this is particularly important in winter when young growing roots and root-hairs may be lacking.

Functional root hairs and other surface cells of the root in contact with soil particles will absorb water as long as the potential of water in the vacuoles is lower than that of the soil solution. Absorption of water by the surface cells leads to an increase in their water potential which results in transfer of water to neighbouring more deeply seated cells having a lower water potential. If no other factors were operative the root would eventually come to equilibrium with the soil solution, when the potential of water in each of the cells was equal to that of the surrounding medium (see Chapter 4, p. 27).

Such an equilibrium is not established in an intact root system because a water-potential difference is maintained between the soil solution and the liquid in the dead conducting elements (vessels and tracheids) in the xylem of the stele. This difference occurs for two reasons:

(i) There is a higher concentration of osmotically active substances in the xylem sap than in the external solution, which causes the sap to have a lower osmotic potential.

(ii) In a transpiring plant, due to evaporation of water from the leaves, a negative pressure (tension) develops in the xylem which is transmitted down the stem and results in lowering of the water potential in the xylem of the root.

The relative importance of these two factors in maintaining a water potential difference across the root cortex will be discussed below.

It is important to appreciate that although a difference of osmotic potential between the soil solution and xylem sap contributes to water movement across the root, *movement through the cortex is in response to a water-potential gradient.* Many students make the mistake of supposing that movement across the cortex depends on the osmotic potential of cells decreasing progressively (that is, becoming more negative) from the root surface inwards. This is not correct! It is a gradient of water potential that is involved, and there is *no* evidence that the osmotic potential of inner cortical cells is significantly lower than that of the surface cells.

So far we have considered the cell to cell movement of water across the root. This is the pathway represented by R_{co_1} in Fig. 7–1. An additional pathway for water movement across the cortex, represented by R_{co_2}, is along the water-filled spaces in the cell walls. These form a continuous system from the water films surrounding soil particles to the endodermis. At this point, the pathway is blocked by the presence of suberized regions (Casparian bands) in the radial and transverse walls, and water taking this route must now join the other pathway. In the older parts of roots, the endodermal cell walls may become completely suberized, except for so-called *passage cells* through which water movement is presumed to occur.

The relative importance of the two pathways across the cortex depends upon the relative values of R_{co_1} and R_{co_2}. If R_{co_1} is a half of R_{co_2} then twice as much water will move across the cortex from cell to cell as through the walls. Unfortunately, it has not yet proved possible to obtain accurate values for R_{co_1} and R_{co_2} and experts disagree about the relative importance of the two pathways. KRAMER (1933) applied reduced pressures by means of a suction pump to the root systems of plants after removal of the shoot and observed that water flowed much more readily through the system when the roots were killed than when they were alive. This is understandable since both R_{st} and R_{co_1} will be drastically reduced when the cells' membranes are rendered more permeable through killing the cells, but it tells us nothing about the values of R_{co_1} and R_{co_2}. LEVITT (1956) concluded on theoretical grounds that osmotic movement of water from cell to cell is much too slow to supply water to the stele at the rate which occurs in a rapidly transpiring plant, and suggested that water movement across the root occurs mainly by mass-flow from the soil via water-filled spaces in cell walls. According to this view, the role of the root system in absorption is mainly that of producing a large absorptive surface in contact with the soil water.

MEES and WEATHERLEY (1957) measured the rates of water movement through excised root systems of tomato plants induced by applying mechanical pressure and by changing the osmotic potential of the outer medium. From a study of the effects of osmotic potential in off-setting mechanical pressure, they concluded that with pressure gradients of up to 2 atm, 75 per cent of the flux was osmotic and 25 per cent by mass flow. Larger mechanical pressures than 2 atm. caused a considerable increase in the osmotic flux. This suggests that negative pressures developed in the xylem through transpiration cause a reduction in R_{co_1} but how it happens is unknown. Low temperature and metabolic inhibitors both increase R_{co_1}, presumably because of a reduction in the permeability of cell protoplasts by these treatments (see p. 35). These effects are difficult to explain on the basis of LEVITT's hypothesis.

7.4   Root pressure and guttation

As has already been indicated, the osmotic potential of the solution in the conducting elements of the xylem is often lower than that of the external medium. This is due to the presence of dissolved inorganic and organic substances, a part of which was accumulated actively in the vacuoles of the conducting elements while they were still alive and the rest transferred subsequently from the living cells surrounding the mature elements. The extent to which these processes lower the osmotic potential of the xylem sap depends not only on the intensity of the accumulation processes, but also on the amount of water which is passing into the xylem. The concentration of dissolved substances in the sap is low when a plant is transpiring actively and high when it is not (RUSSELL and BARBER, 1960). It is for this reason that the *quantity* of dissolved substances, such as mineral salts, carried upwards into the shoot in the transpiration stream is largely independent of the rate of transpiration.

The osmotic potential of xylem sap falls to its lowest level in a de-shooted plant because then water absorption is minimal. If a manometer is connected to the cut stump of a potted plant such as a *Fuchsia* the development of 'root pressure', caused by osmotic absorption of water into the xylem can readily be demonstrated. This activity is very intense in certain plants under favourable conditions and notably so in vines. HALES reported in Vegetable Staticks (1727) that when he attached a ¼ in. diameter tube to a cut vine stem, liquid rose in it to a height of 21 feet over a period of several days and 'would very probably have risen higher if the joynt had not several times leaked'. He noticed that the level of the liquid rose much more quickly during the day than at night. This diurnal periodicity in root pressure has been confirmed by later investigations and is sometimes cited as evidence that metabolic processes are directly involved in water absorption by roots (e.g. GROSSENBACHER, 1938). What actually happens is that there is a rhythm in the intensity of accumulation of dissolved substances in the xylem sap which is linked to fluctuating metabolic activity and this affects water absorption indirectly (ARISZ, HELDER and VAN NIE, 1951; VAADIA, 1960). As may be expected, root pressure is reduced by lowering the temperature, by withholding inorganic nutrients and by metabolic inhibitors. It is stimulated by auxins for reasons which are still not clear.

Positive pressures are developed sometimes in the xylem of intact plants and are largely responsible for the phenomenon of 'guttation'—the release of liquid water from leaves. Guttation can be demonstrated readily by placing young seedlings (oat, maize and other grass seedlings work well) under a bell jar in a warm laboratory. The liquid emerges either from stomata or from 'water pores' (hydathodes) situated at the edges of the leaves. Often it appears merely to take the pathway of least resistance from the vein endings in the leaf. It is possible that some hydathodes excrete water actively (so-called 'active' hydathodes) but evidence for this is still uncertain. Many plants in tropical rain forests guttate profusely and to stand beneath one of them is said to be like being out in gentle rain. Guttation is generally more active at night, presumably because the positive pressure in the xylem is highest at the time when transpiration is least.

7.5   The pathway of water transport

In the discussion so far it has been assumed that water is carried upwards in the stem through the non-living xylem elements, that is through *vessels* (which only occur in angiosperms) and *tracheids*. Anatomically, these elements appear to be admirably suited for the purpose (Fig. 7–4). In the case of vessels, the transverse walls separating each vessel-segment from its neighbours disappear during development leaving only a series of rims to indicate their former location, and causing the establishment of continuous tubes from the roots to the leaves. The pathway for water through a system of tracheids is more circuitous than through vessels but continuity is established between one element and the next via the characteristic bordered pits (Fig. 7–4). As may be expected, tracheids offer a higher resistance to the flow of water along them than do vessels, and this can be demonstrated readily by comparing the rates of flow of water through lengths of twig of similar diameter under the influence of a pressure gradient. Deciduous angiosperm

6—P.W.

tree wood has a specific conductivity which is commonly 3–6 times higher than that of conifers.

Another indication that xylem is the tissue involved in the movement of water in stems is that there is a close correlation between the amount of xylem associated with individual leaves and the quantity of water they transpire. As already mentioned (p. 2) the number of vessels and tracheids is reduced in submerged water plants, but when leaves emerge from the water, e.g. in the water plantain (*Alisma plantago-aquatica*) they are well supplied with xylem.

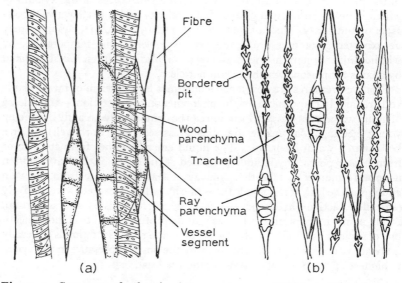

Fibre

Bordered pit

Wood parenchyma

Tracheid

Ray parenchyma

Vessel segment

(a)   (b)

Fig. 7–4   Structure of xylem in: (a) an angiosperm (*Tilia*), and (b) a gymnosperm (*Pinus*) as seen in longitudinal section.

More direct evidence that the xylem is involved in longitudinal transport comes from the following observations:

(i) When the cut end of a stem is placed in an aqueous solution of dye, e.g. eosin, the liquid is taken up, and subsequent microscopic observation reveals that, except near the cut surface where there is general staining of the cells, only the walls of the xylem vessels and tracheids are coloured. This shows that, at least in cut shoots, the vessels and tracheids offer a path of least resistance to aqueous solutions. This observation does not prove, as is sometimes claimed, that xylem is also the tissue involved in water transport in the intact plant, but experiments in which intact seedlings are placed with their roots in solutions of dye yield similar results. Near the root tip, the whole meristem becomes uniformly coloured, but elsewhere staining is particularly evident in the walls of the tracheids and vessels.

Similar experiments have been performed using water containing a radio-active substance, the location of the radioactivity being determined subsequently by autoradiography. Such experiments like those with dyes are open to the criticism that water and dissolved substances do not necessarily travel in the stem by the same path. This objection can be overcome by the use of isotopically labelled water (BIDDULPH, NAKAYANA and CORY, 1961).

(ii) The importance of tissues central to the bark in the movement of water through stems can be demonstrated quite simply by '*ringing*' *experiments*. If a zone of bark is removed from the stem, transport of water continues apparently unaffected, at least for a time, but if a section of xylem is removed with minimum disturbance of the bark the plant wilts rapidly. This kind of observation does not provide information as to the precise cells involved in water movement.

The great German plant physiologist of the nineteenth century, JULIUS SACHS, suggested that water might be transported through the stems of plants by capillarity in the walls of the vessels and tracheids rather than in the lumina. The inadequacy of this hypothesis can be demonstrated by an experiment in which the cavities of the xylem elements are occluded with a substance, e.g. paraffin wax, which is impermeable to water. It can be shown by incorporating fat-soluble dyes, e.g. sudan 3, into the wax that the impregnating material does not penetrate the spaces in the walls of the conducting elements, and yet the movement of water through the xylem is restricted. Another observation conflicting with SACHS's proposal is that in plants with flexible stems, e.g. vines, flow of water can be prevented by applying sufficient mechanical pressure to close the cavities of the xylem elements. It is unlikely that such a treatment affects significantly the size of the spaces in the walls.

The fact that water apparently moves up the stem through *dead* xylem elements implies that *living cells* in the stem are not directly involved in the transport process. The best evidence in support of this comes from experiments similar to that performed by STRASBURGER (1891) which show that after the living cells adjoining the xylem have been killed by poison, a stem still conducts water. He cut across the base of a young oak tree and immersed the cut end in a barrel of picric acid. After allowing time for the transport of the poison into the leaves, he replaced the solution by water containing a dye. Subsequent observations showed that the dye ascended quickly into the leaves.

If a section of a stem is killed by heat or by application of metabolic poisons, the leaves above eventually wilt. DIXON (1914) argued convincingly that this effect is an indirect one resulting from a blocking of the conducting elements by substances derived from the dead cells. HANDLEY (1939) observed that application of low temperatures to a section of stem of an intact plant caused it to wilt. He attributed this to interference with metabolism of cells adjoining the xylem, but more recently ZIMMERMANN (1965) has shown that water movement is only affected if temperatures are low enough to cause the xylem sap to freeze.

The presence of living cells in the stem is, of course, *indirectly* necessary for water movement in so far as the conducting elements function for a relatively short time (see below) and their continuous replacement depends on the activity of living cambial cells adjoining them.

7.6   Velocity of flow

The quantity of water (Q) transported through a stem in unit time can be calculated from the formula $Q = Av$, where A is the cross-sectional area of the cavities through which transport occurs and v is the linear velocity.

Q can be estimated from transpiration determinations and if v is known the cross-sectional area of the functional channels in the xylem may be calculated. SACHS (1887) attempted to measure v by observing the rate of

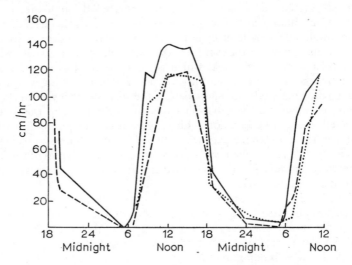

Fig. 7–5   Diurnal variation in the rate of sap movement in *Larix* (———), *Picea* (– – – – –) and *Fagus* (·······). (HUBER and SCHMIDT, 1937)

transport of lithium ions, which can be detected conveniently by a flame test, through the stems of intact plants after lithium nitrate had been applied to the roots. Fluorescent dyes and radioactive substances have been used since in a similar way. After supplying ^{32}P-labelled phosphate in the nutrient solution ARNON, STOUT and SIPOS (1940) found that radioactivity was detectable in the upper leaves of tall tomato plants under conditions of high transpiration after 40 minutes. It should be emphasized that the velocities recorded in such experiments are influenced by the sensitivity of the method used for detecting the indicator in the upper parts of the plant. It is assumed that water is transported upwards through the stem at the same velocity as the indicator substances supplied, which may not be the case.

An ingenious thermo-electric method, originally used to measure the rate of circulation of blood, was developed by HUBER and SCHMIDT (1937) to estimate the rate of flow of the transpiration stream in trees. The method involves brief application of heat to a localized region of the stem, and measurement by means of sensitive thermocouples of the rate of its subsequent transfer upwards and downwards from the point of application. From the difference in the time taken for the heat to be transferred in the two directions, the rate of movement of the transpiration stream in the superficial elements can be calculated. Rates varying from near zero to over 100 cm per hour were recorded depending on the time of day at which the observations were made (Fig. 7–5). HUBER and SCHMIDT found that there was a gradual lowering in velocity from the base to the apex of trees. This was attributed to an increase in the total effective cross-sectional area for conduction in the upper parts of the plant.

A study of the relationship between the amounts of water loss by a plant and the rates of linear flow indicate that in ring-porous trees, such as ash and oak, where the spring wood contains a number of large vessels, movement of water longitudinally is mainly in the outermost annual ring. The large vessels which carry most of the water seem to function only during the season in which they are formed, being replaced by new vessels associated with the new crop of leaves in the following season. In diffuse-porous trees, e.g. sycamore, the spring vessels are smaller and appear to function for several years.

7.7   Mechanisms of water movement

A variety of mechanisms contribute to the movement of water through a stem. One of these is *root pressure* (see p. 66), as a result of which water is forced upwards along a hydrostatic pressure gradient. The magnitude of root pressure rarely exceeds a few atmospheres, but this is sufficient to supply water to the leaves in slowly transpiring herbaceous plants. To move water from the base to the leaves of the tallest trees, over 300 feet in height, pressures of up to 40 atm are required, and root pressures of this order of magnitude have not been detected. In fact in rapidly transpiring trees the water in the xylem is commonly under tension, as is shown by the fact that water is absorbed when it is poured on to the root-stump of a newly-felled tree. For these reasons root pressure cannot be considered to be of foremost importance in the movement of water in trees.

Capillarity

Water can rise to an appreciable height in fine capillary tubes because of its high surface tension. In a glass tube of 0·01 mm bore, water will rise by capillarity to a height of about 3 metres. The diameter of conducting elements in xylem varies from rather less than 0·01 mm for some gymnosperm tracheids to 0·2 mm for the largest vessels in ring-porous trees. Clearly water will not rise by capillarity in the lumina of these vessels to a height sufficient to supply tall trees. SACHS (1887) pointed out that water might rise to great heights by capillarity if it moved in the narrow spaces between the cellulose fibres in cell walls, as in a wick. However, experiments have shown that the resistance of cell walls to water movement is so high that they cannot transmit water at the necessary rate to prevent wilting (see p. 69).

Reduced atmospheric pressure

The suggestion has been made at various times that water might be moved through the stems of plants by reduced atmospheric pressure, in the same way as the liquid rises in a barometer. It has been observed that vessels sometimes contain gas at reduced pressure (see below) but even if the air pressure were reduced to zero above a water column, the water would not rise to a greater height than about 34 feet (i.e. equivalent to 1 atm pressure difference).

Cohesion hypothesis

The close relationship between transpiration and the rate of movement of water in stems suggests that evaporation is involved somehow in the mechanism of water transport. One way in which this might occur can be explained by reference to the physical model illustrated in Fig. 7–6. As water evaporates from the porous surface, capillary forces maintain the position of the water menisci in the pores causing reduced pressure inside the pot. In such a system a mercury column has been caused to rise to greater heights than can occur by reduced atmospheric pressure.

BOEHM (1892) demonstrated that the same thing happens when the porous pot is replaced by a transpiring shoot, and he suggested that water is moved into the leaves of plants in a similar way as a result of transpiration. This idea was elaborated by DIXON and JOLY (1894) and by ASKENASY (1895) and has become known as the *cohesion hypothesis*. According to the proposal, evaporation of water from the surface of the mesophyll cells in the leaf causes a reduction in their water potential and this instigates withdrawal of water from the ends of the conducting elements, with which they are in contact via water-filled cell walls. The water in the xylem is thus placed under a tension which is transmitted downwards because of the cohesive properties of continuous water columns existing in the vessels and tracheids between the leaf and the roots of the plant. The reduced pressure in the xylem elements of the root causes entry of water (see Chapter 6) and the whole column moves upwards by mass flow. The development of tensions in the xylem of transpiring trees is indicated by the fact that the diameter of the stem contracts slightly when transpiration occurs, as can be shown by fixing a suitable caliper ('dendrograph', MACDOUGAL, 1925) to the tree-trunk.

There are two major conditions which must exist in the plant if the cohesion hypothesis is valid:

1. the pressure gradient developed as a result of evaporation must be sufficient to move water at the rates which occur, and
2. continuous columns of water must exist between the evaporating surfaces and the roots of the plant.

The hypothesis has been criticized on both these grounds.

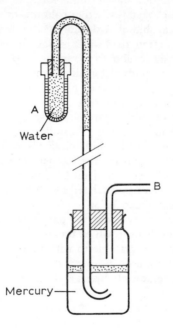

Fig. 7–6 The cohesion hypothesis. A demonstration that evaporation can raise water to a height greater than is possible by atmospheric pressure. It is essential that the water in the porous pot, A, and connecting tube is free of air. This can be accomplished by surrounding A with a beaker of boiling water, and allowing excess water and air to escape from B. When the beaker is removed evaporation from A causes the level of mercury in the tube to rise to a height which may exceed 76 cm.

With regard to the force required, the most recent calculations (ZIMMERMANN, 1965) indicate that a pressure gradient of about 0·15 atm per metre is required for water movement at peak velocity in a variety of tree species. This would be equivalent to a water potential difference of about 40 atm in the case of the tallest trees. Water potentials of this order have been recorded for leaf cells. It may be significant that there is a tendency for tree leaves to have lower (i.e. more negative) water potentials than those of shrubs and herbs, and that leaves near the tops of trees commonly have the lowest water-potential values of all. The height of the tallest trees (e.g. some of the giant Redwoods in California, and Eucalyptus in Australia) may be limited by the maximum water potential which can be developed in the uppermost leaves, but it is evident that in general an adequate water-potential gradient is available.

Most of the discussion about the validity of the cohesion hypothesis centres round the question of continuity of the water system. The first question which may be asked is whether columns of water in the cavities of xylem elements are capable of withstanding the tensions which must be developed. The tensile strength of water is high and FISHER (1948) estimated that theoretically a tension of about 1300 atm is necessary to break a stretched water column. Experimentally determined values for water and expressed xylem sap are much lower than this, ranging from about 25 atm to over 300 atm in different investigations (see e.g. LOOMIS, SANTAMARIA and GAGE, 1960). Determinations of tensile strength have usually been made by Berthelot's method. This involves filling a capillary tube with the solution and then sealing it to leave a small bubble of air inside saturated with vapour. The liquid is expanded by raising the temperature until it completely fills the tube and then it is allowed to cool until the bubble reappears. The tension developed in the tube can be calculated from the change in volume of the water and its coefficient of expansion.

In spite of the uncertainty about the tensile strength of xylem sap, especially under the conditions in which it exists in the plant, it may be concluded that water columns are able to withstand the tensions likely to be developed during transpiration at least for a time. There will undoubtedly be a tendency for the columns to break and this will be most likely to occur in the largest vessels.

The cohesion hypothesis has been criticized also on the grounds that xylem vessels are filled not with continuous columns of water under tension but with air and water vapour under reduced pressure (PRESTON, 1952). There is no doubt that even in undisturbed plants a considerable proportion of the conducting elements are filled with gas. In the case of trees, the density of wood and its water content vary enormously throughout the year being high in spring and early summer and low in the autumn. This has important implications in the lumber industry, since when the water content is high, the logs may be so dense that they will not float. The presence of air in even a high percentage of the conducting channels does not necessarily invalidate the cohesion hypothesis, since only a small number of elements need to be functional at any time to supply the needs of the plant (p. 71).

In cases where plant stems are transparent enough for direct observation, one can see that at least some of the vessels are water-filled, even under conditions of severe wilting. In trees, direct evidence of existing water columns has been obtained by freezing the trunks rapidly, and sectioning them in a frozen state for microscopy (ZIMMERMANN, 1965). The presence of clear ice in the sectioned vessels is taken to indicate that they were filled with water when the tree was felled.

An observation which is difficult at first sight to reconcile with the cohesion hypothesis is that when two overlapping cuts are made from opposite sides of a tree in leaf (Fig. 7-7) it can survive if precautions are taken to support it, and it may not even wilt although all the water columns in the stem have evidently been broken. The explanation that is given of this on the basis of the cohesion hypothesis is that there is a sufficient reservoir of water above the cuts to supply the leaves, until new intact conducting elements have been formed round the cuts by renewed cambial activity. Alternatively, the

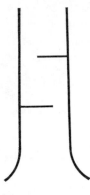

Fig. 7-7   An experiment to test the validity of the cohesion hypothesis. For explanation, see text.

conducting element above the cuts may draw water laterally from neighbouring living cells which are interconnected round the cuts to other parenchyma cells and via them to conducting elements below. The effect of the cuts may then only be to increase the overall resistance of the pathway for water movement, the continuity of water columns being maintained via water-filled spaces in the cell walls of intervening parenchyma cells. There is no doubt that there is a continual exchange of water between the conducting elements and the surrounding cells even in the intact system. The living cells act as a reservoir of water within the plant which is depleted to some extent in deciduous trees during periods of rapid transpiration and refilled during the winter. At this time some of the conducting elements in which the water columns have been broken may be refilled too and become functional again in the next season.

Although the original concept was no doubt over-simplified, the essential basis of cohesion hypothesis has stood up well to critical investigation for nearly three-quarters of a century. When due account is taken of the structural complexity of the water conducting system in plants it appears to be a plausible mechanism for water movement in stems and it provides the only adequate explanation of sap ascent in tall trees.

Further Reading

General

CRAFTS, A. B., CURRIER, H. B. and STOCKING, C. R. (1949). *Water in the Physiology of Plants*. Ronald, New York.
KOZLOWSKI, T. T. (1964). *Water Metabolism in Plants*. Harper Row, New York.
KRAMER, P. J. (1949). *Plant and Soil Water Relations*. McGraw-Hill, New York and Maidenhead.
RUTTER, A. J. and WHITEHEAD, F. H., eds. (1963). *The Water Relations of Plants*. Blackwell Scientific, Oxford.
SLATYER, R. O. (1967). *Plant–Water Relationships*. Academic Press, New York and London.
SLAVIK, B., ed. (1965). *Water Stress in Plants*. Junk, The Hague.

Chapter 1

ARBER, A. (1925). *Water Plants*. Cambridge University Press, London.
DAUBENMIRE, R. F. (1959). *Plants and Environment*. 2nd edition. Wiley, New York.
MAXIMOV, N. A. (1929). *The Plant in Relation to Water*, edited by R. H. YAPP. English Translation. Allen and Unwin, London.
RAUNKIAEV, C. (1937). *Plant Life Forms*, translated by M. GILBERT-CARTER. Oxford.

Chapter 2

BERNAL, J. D. (1965). *Society for Experimental Biology Symposia*, **19**, 17.
KLOTZ, I. M. (1962). *Horizons in Biochemistry*, edited by M. KASHA and B. PULLMAN, p. 523. Academic Press, New York and London.
HENDERSON, L. J. (1913). *The Fitness of the Environment*. Macmillan, London and New York.

Chapter 3

DICK, D. A. T. (1966). *Cell Water*, Chapter 3. Butterworths, London.
EDSALL, J. T. and WYMAN, J. (1958). *Biophysical Chemistry*, vol. 1. Academic Press, New York and London.
HILDEBRANDT, J. H. (1955). *Science*, N.Y., **121**, 116.
KRAMER, P. J., KNIPLING, E. B. and MILLER, L. N. (1966). *Science*, N.Y., **153**, 889.

Chapter 4

BENNET-CLARK, T. A. (1959). *Plant Physiology*, edited by F. C. STEWARD. Vol. 2, Chapter 2, p. 105. Academic Press, New York and London.
DAINTY, J. (1963). *Advances in Botanical Research*, Vol. 1, p. 279. Academic Press, New York and London.
KRAMER, P. J. (1955). *Annual Review of Plant Physiology*, **6**, 253.
SLATYER, R. O. (1962). *Annual Review of Plant Physiology*, **13**, 351.

Chapter 5

HEATH, O. V. S. (1959). *Plant Physiology*, edited by F. C. STEWARD. Vol. 2, Chapter 3, p. 193. Academic Press, New York and London.

KETELLAPER, H. J. (1963). *Annual Review of Plant Physiology*, **14**, 249.

MEIDNER H. and MANSFIELD, T. A. (1968). *Physiology of Stomata*, McGraw-Hill, New York and London.

PENMAN, H. L. (1942). *Proceedings of the Royal Society, London Series B*, **130**, 416.

ZELITCH, I., ed. (1963). *Stomata and Water Relations in Plants*. Connecticut Agricultural Experimental Station Bulletin 664.

Chapter 6

HALES, S. (1727). *Vegetable Staticks*. Oldbourne, London (1961 edition).

KRAMER, P. J. (1959). *Plant Physiology*, edited by F. C. STEWARD. Vol. 2, Chapter 7, p. 607. Academic Press, New York and London.

MEIDNER, H. (1965). *Society for Experimental Biology Symposia*, **19**, 185.

MONTEITH, J. L. (1965). *Society for Experimental Biology Symposia*, **19**, 205.

PENMAN, H. L. (1963). *Commonwealth Agricultural Bureau of Soils, Technical Communication* 53, Farnham Royal, England.

Chapter 7

DIXON, H. H. (1914). *Transpiration and the Ascent of Sap in Plants*. Macmillan, London.

GREENIDGE, K. N. H. (1957). *Annual Review of Plant Physiology*, **8**, 237.

ZIMMERMANN, M. H. (1965). *Society for Experimental Biology Symposia*, **19**, 151.

References

ALVIM, P. DE T. and HAVIS, J. R. (1954). *Pl. Physiol., Lancaster*, **29**, 97.
ANDERSSON, N. E., HERTZ, C. H. and RUFELT, H. (1954). *Physiologia Pl.*, **7**, 753.
ARBER, A. (1925). *Water Plants*. Cambridge University Press, London.
ARISZ, W. H., HELDER, R. J. and VAN NIE, R. (1951). *J. exp. Bot.*, **2**, 257.
ARNON, D. I., STOUT, P. R. and SIPOS, F. (1940). *Am. J. Bot.*, **27**, 791.
ASKENASY, E. (1895). *Bot. Zbl.*, **62**, 237.
BALDES, E. J. and JOHNSON, A. F. (1939). *Biodynamica*, **2**, 1.
BANGE, G. G. J. (1953). *Acta. bot. neerl.*, **2**, 255.
BENNET-CLARK, T. A., GREENWOOD, A. D. and BARKER, J. W. (1936). *New Phytol.*, **35**, 277.
BERNAL, J. D. (1965). *Symp. Soc. exp. Biol.*, **19**, 17.
BIDDULPH, O., NAKAYAMA, F. S. and CORY, R. (1961). *Pl. Physiol., Lancaster*, **36**, 429.
BIERHUIZEN, J. F., SLATYER, R. O. and ROSE, C. W. (1965). *J. exp. Bot.*, **16**, 182.
BOEHM, E. (1892). *Ber. dt. bot. Ges.*, **10**, 539.
BRAUNER, L. (1930). *Ber. dt. bot. Ges.*, **48**, 109.
BRIGGS, L. J. and SHANTZ, H. L. (1916). *J. agric. Res.*, **7**, 155.
BROWN, H. T. and ESCOMBE, F. (1900). *Phil. Trans. R. Soc. B*, **193**, 223.
DAINTY, J. and GINZBURG, B. Z. (1964). *Biochem. biophys. Acta*, **79**, 102.
DANIELLI, J. F. (1954). *Symp. Soc. exp. Biol.*, **8**, 502.
DARWIN, F. and PERTZ, D. F. M. (1911). *Proc. R. Soc. B*, **84**, 136.
DECKER, J. P. and WIEN, J. D. (1960). *Pl. Physiol., Lancaster*, **35**, 340.
DIXON, H. (1914). *Transpiration and the Ascent of Sap*. Macmillian, London.
DIXON, H. H. and JOLY, J. (1894). *Ann Bot.*, **8**, 468.
FALK, S. O. (1966). *Z. Pflphysiol.*, **55**, 31.
FISHER, J. C. (1948). *J. appl. Phys.*, **19**, 1062.
FREEMAN, G. F. (1908). *Bot. Gaz.*, **46**, 118.
GLOVER, J. (1941). *Ann. Bot. N.S.*, **5**, 25.
GREGORY, F. G., MILTHORPE, F. L., PEARSE, H. L. and SPENCER, H. J. (1950). *J. exp. Bot.*, **1**, 15.
GREGORY, F. G. and PEARSE, H. L. (1934). *Proc. R. Soc. B*, **114**, 477.
GROSSENBACHER, K. A. (1938). *Pl. Physiol., Lancaster*, **13**, 669.
HAAN, I. DE (1933), *Recl. trav. botan. néerl.*, **30**, 234.
HANDLEY, W. R. C. (1939). *Ann Bot. N.S.*, **3**, 803.
HANES, C. S. (1940). *Nature, Lond.*, **145**, 348.
HEATH, O. V. S. (1952). *New Phytol.*, **51**, 30.
HEATH, O. V. S. (1959). *Plant Physiology*, edited by F. C. STEWARD. Vol. 2, p. 193. Academic Press, New York.
HEATH, O. V. S. and ORCHARD, B. (1956). *J. exp. Bot.*, **7**, 313.
HEATH, O. V. S. and RUSSELL, J. (1951). *J. exp. Bot.*, **2**, 111.
HÖFLER, K. (1917). *Ber. dt. bot. Ges.*, **55**, 514.
HUBER, B. (1927). *Ber. dt. bot. Ges.*, **45**, 611.
HUBER, B. (1953). *Forstwiss. ZentBl.*, **72**, 257.
HUBER, B. and HÖFLER, K. (1930). *Jb. wiss. Bot.*, **73**, 351.

HUBER, B. and SCHMIDT, E. (1937). *Ber. dt. bot. Ges.*, **55**, 514.

KAMIYA, N. and TAZAWA, M. (1956). *Protoplasma*, **46**, 394.

KOHN, P. G. (1965). *Symp. Soc. exp. Biol.*, **19**, 3.

KRAMER, P. J. (1933). *Am. J. Bot.*, **20**, 481.

KRAMER, P. J. (1949). *Plant and Soil Water Relationships*. McGraw-Hill, New York and Maidenhead.

KNIGHT, R. C. (1915). *New Phytol.*, **14**, 212.

LEVITT, J. (1947). *Pl. Physiol.*, *Lancaster*, **22**, 514.

LEVITT, J. (1956). *Pl. Physiol.*, *Lancaster*, **31**, 248.

LEVITT, J., SCARTH, G. W. and GIBBS, R. D. (1936). *Protoplasma*, **26**, 237.

LLOYD, F. E. (1908). *Publs. Carnegie Instn.*, **82**, 1.

LOOMIS, W. E., SANTAMARIA, R. and GAGE, R. S. (1960). *Pl. Physiol.*, *Lancaster*, **35**, 300.

MACDOUGAL, D. T. (1925). *Publs. Carnegie Instn.*, **365**, 1.

MEES, G. C. and WEATHERLEY, P. E. (1957). *Proc. R. Soc. B*, **147**, 381.

MEIDNER, H. (1965). *Sch. Sci. Rev.*, **16**, 149.

MEYER, B. S. (1945). *Pl. Physiol.*, *Lancaster*, **20**, 142.

MEYER, B. S. and WALLACE, A. M. (1941). *Am. J. Bot.*, **28**, 838.

MYERS, G. M. P. (1951). *J. exp. Bot.*, **2**, 129.

MILLER, E. C. (1938). *Plant Physiology*, 2nd edition. McGraw-Hill, New York.

MILTHORPE, F. L. (1955). *J. exp. Bot.*, **6**, 17.

MOLISCH, H. (1912). *Z. Bot.*, **4**, 106.

OGATA, G., RICHARDS, L. A. and GARDNER, W. R. (1960). *Soil Sci.*, **89**, 179.

PENMAN, H. L. (1948). *Proc. R. Soc. A*, **193**, 120.

PFEFFER, W. F. P. (1877). *Osmotische Untersuchungen*. Engelmann, Leipzig.

PRESTON, R. D. (1952). *Deformation and Flow in Biological Systems*. Edited by FREY-WYSSLING, A. North Holland, Amsterdam.

PULVA, P. (1939). *Protoplasma*, **32**, 265.

RESÜHR, B. (1935). *Protoplasma*, **24**, 531.

RICHARDS, B. G. (1965). *Nature, Lond.*, **208**, 608.

RICHARDS, L. A. (1949). *Soil Sci.*, **68**, 95.

RICHARDS, L. A. and OGATA, G. (1958). *Science, N.Y.*, **128**, 1089.

RUSSELL, R. S. and BARBER, D. A. (1960). *A. Rev. Pl. Physiol.*, **11**, 127.

SACHS, J. (1887). *Lectures on the Physiology of Plants*, English edition. Clarendon Press, Oxford.

SAYRE, J. D. (1926). *Ohio J. Sci.*, **26**, 233.

SCARTH, G. W., LOEWY, A. and SHAW, M. (1948). *Can. J. Res.*, C26, 94.

SCARTH, G. W. and SHAW, M. (1951). *Pl. Physiol.*, *Lancaster*, **26**, 581.

SCHOLANDER, P. F. (1955). *Pl. Physiol.*, *Lancaster*, **30**, 506.

SHAW, M. and MACLACHLAN, G. A. (1954). *Can. J. Bot.*, **32**, 784.

SHIMSHI, D. and LIVINE, A. (1967). *Ann. Bot.* N.S., **31**, 505.

SPANNER, D. G. (1951). *J. exp. Bot.*, **2**, 145.

SPANNER, D. G. and HEATH, O. V. S. (1951). *Ann. Bot.* N.S., **15**, 319.

STEFAN, J. (1881). *Sber. Akad. Wiss. Wien*, **68**, 385.

STOCKER, O. (1956). *Encyclopaedia of Plant Physiology*, edited by W. RUHLAND. Vol. 3, 293. Springer, Berlin.

STOCKING, C. R. (1945). *Am. J. Bot.*, **32**, 126.

STRASBURGER, E. (1891). *Ueber der Bau und die Verrichtungen der Leitsbahnen in der Pflantzen*. Fischer, Jena.

TAMIYA, H. (1938). *Cytologia, Tokyo*, **8**, 542.

THIMANN, K. V. and SAMUEL, E. W. (1955). *Proc. nat. Acad. Sci.*, **41**, 1029.

TURRELL, F. M. (1944). *Bot. Gaz.*, **105**, 413.

URSPRUNG, A. and BLUM, G. (1916). *Ber. dtsch. bot. Ges.*, **34**, 88.

VAADIA, Y. (1960). *Physiol. Pl.*, **13**, 701.

VERDUIN, J. (1949). In *Photosynthesis*, edited by J. FRANCK and W. E. LOOMIS. Iowa State College, Ames, Iowa.

WADLEIGH, C. H. and AYERS, A. D. (1945). *Pl. Physiol.*, *Lancaster*, **20**, 106.

WEINTRAUB, M. (1952). *New Phytol.*, **50**, 357.

WILLIAMS, W. T. (1949). *Ann. Bot.* N.S., **13**, 309.

WILLIAMS, W. T. (1954). *J. exp. Bot.*, **5**, 343.

YIN, H. C. and TUNG, Y. T. (1948). *Science, N.Y.*, **108**, 98.

YEMM, E. W. and WILLIS, A. J. (1954). *New Phytol.*, **53**, 373.

ZIMMERMANN, M. H. (1965). *Symp. Soc. exp. Biol.*, **19**, 151